DEDICATION

This book is dedicated to the most inspiring woman I have ever known — my precious wife, Sandra, who makes every day a joy. Without her continuing encouragement, support, and unconditional love I am certain I would accomplish little in this life!

Salvation is the greatest gift ever given to mankind, but the love of a godly woman is a close second.

This book is highly recommended by:

> "This book will not only inform you, it will inspire you and challenge you to increased evangelistic consciousness, greater missionary concern, and a desire to live a holy life in an unholy age."

— **Tim LaHaye**, co-author of New York Times Best Seller *Left Behind*

> "Gary Frazier's passion in life is motivating followers of Christ regarding the return of Jesus. He communicates the prophetic Word with urgency and clarity!"

— **Charles Stanley,** author and Senior Pastor, First Baptist Church, Atlanta, GA

Do you want to know how biblical prophecy is impacting your world? Allow Dr. Gary Frazier to separate fact from fiction for you.

Dr. Frazier, president of Discovery Missions, is a respected speaker and author of Bible prophecy and current events who has appeared on numerous documentaries, the History Channel, and national radio programs. He is the author of numerous books and is a contributor to the LaHaye *Prophecy Study Bible* and *The Popular Encyclopedia of Bible Prophecy*. He travels nationally, speaking in many of America's largest churches. Frazier attended Criswell College, Southwestern Seminary, and Louisiana Baptist University, holding several graduate degrees.

Meet the Author via video!
Scan this code with your
smart phone or go to
nlpg.com/**itcouldhappen**

T COULD HAPPEN TOMORROW

FUTURE

EVENTS

THAT WILL

SHAKE THE

WORLD

GARY FRAZIER

…helps us understand the wonderful plan God has for our future, both now on this earth and in the life hereafter.
—Tim LaHaye, co-author of New York Times Bestselling Series Left Behind

First printing: January 2012
Second printing: June 2012

Copyright © 2011 by Gary Frazier. All rights reserved. No part of this book may be used or reproduced in any manner whatsoever without written permission of the publisher, except in the case of brief quotations in articles and reviews. For information write:
New Leaf Press, P.O. Box 726, Green Forest, AR 72638
New Leaf Press is a division of the New Leaf Publishing Group, Inc.

ISBN: 978-0-89221-711-3
Library of Congress Number: 2011945209

Cover by Diana Bogardus

Please consider requesting that a copy of this volume be purchased by your local library system.

Printed in the United States of America

Please visit our website for other great titles:
www.newleafpress.net

For information regarding author interviews,
please contact the publicity department at (870) 438-5288.

New Leaf Press
A Division of New Leaf Publishing Group
www.newleafpress.net

CONTENTS

FOREWORD

One of the best things about being asked to write a foreword to a book by Dr. Gary Frazier is that I get to enjoy reading it before it is published. When it comes to Bible prophecy, he is a good writer, clear and interesting. Gary and I have been friends for several years; in fact, we have spoken together at over 50 prophecy conferences in many of the great churches in the country. He, Dr. Ed Hindson, and I have seen hundreds come to Christ at these meetings and thousands find new meaning and purpose in life.

Studying Bible prophecy has many positive effects on both Christians and unbelievers. It helps us understand the wonderful plan God has for our future, both now on this earth and in the life hereafter. There must be some powerful reason that God made 28 percent of the Bible prophetic when it was first written. And there is! When it is fulfilled it proves beyond doubt that He is GOD. He even says that Himself. Read Isaiah 46:9–10 and you will see that He used fulfilled prophecy to prove that He was the only deity that the children of Israel should worship. For only He could "make known the end from the beginning," and in that context He is pointing out that idols cannot forecast the future, but He does.

The best definition I have seen of true prophecy is "history written in advance," and only God has done that which is recorded over one thousand times in Scripture. According to Dr. John Walvoord, the dean of 20th-century prophecy scholars, he has found over five hundred of those predictions that have already been fulfilled. That is no doubt what the Apostle Peter called "the sure word of prophecy." Why is that important? One fulfilled prophecy would prove God had given it, but over five hundred fulfilled prophecies shrieks at us that the Bible, from which they all come, was inspired by God and is reliable! In fact, I like to think that those over five hundred fulfilled prophecies credential God, His Word, and His Son Jesus Christ (who fulfilled over 109 prophecies, proving He alone was the Messiah), and confirms that salvation comes from Him alone and that we can rely on the yet future prophecies of the end times to be fulfilled in the future, just as He fulfilled those that are now history.

Dr. Frazier uses many of these end-time prophecies to show how our generation could very well be the last generation before the Rapture. Not only does he describe the rapture and the surrounding events, he also puts into perspective the many other key subjects predicted for the near future. These events will cause "thinking" people to believe Jesus' coming back to this earth is not only certain, it could very well be soon.

This book will not only inform you, it will inspire you and challenge you to increased evangelistic consciousness, greater missionary concern, and a desire to live a holy life in an unholy age — something we all need.

Dr. Tim LaHaye Palm Springs, California
co-author of the Left Behind Series

Introduction

FUTURE EVENTS THAT WILL SHAKE THE WORLD

Recently, while sitting in our den and surfing the 102 cable channels that make me crazy, I ran across a commercial that captured my attention. Of all places it was on the Weather Channel. Now I realize that no one under the age of 60 ever watches the Weather Channel, but I was captivated nonetheless. There on the screen, gleaming in the bright sunlight, was San Francisco, the famous Golden Gate Bridge and the beautiful bay. My thoughts raced back to the times my wife, Sandra, and I have spent visiting this destination and the many times we have enjoyed the fantastic sourdough bread in any number of the restaurants along the boardwalk. All of a sudden the picture began to change into a reddish color synonymous with disaster. The announcer's voice came in with this deep ominous tone and said, "The city by the bay, destroyed by a magnitude 9.5 earthquake. . . . It Could Happen Tomorrow!"

Immediately the scene changed to Dallas, Texas, the city of my birth. There on the screen was Reunion Tower glistening in the bright Texas sunlight. Reunion Tower has replaced Southfork Ranch as the most recognized symbol of this great city in the south central part of America. For several years during the Christmas season I would load the family into our Cessna 421 and head south after obtaining permission from air traffic control for low altitude flight, fly my family around downtown Dallas and Reunion Tower. We loved taking in the festive lights of the season. Reunion Tower was always especially beautiful because during the holiday season the blinking lights would change from white to red and green. Now, here on the screen the scene began to change once again to that same reddish color. The announcer stated, "Dallas, Texas, hit by an F5 tornado and is no more. . . . It Could Happen Tomorrow!"

By this time I am sitting on the edge of my seat and my mind is racing with thoughts of the possibilities of these events when the scene changes yet a third time. Manhattan, New York! Everyone recognizes Manhattan as one of the most striking symbols of economic prowess in the world today. Although the Twin Towers are no more, Manhattan is right there with Paris, Rome, London, and Tokyo as one of the great cities of the modern world. Manhattan was glistening in the sun, just as it was on September 11, 2001. Then all of a sudden there was that reddish hue again and the voice said, "Manhattan, with its 14 plus million people, has been hit by a tsunami and is no more. . . . It Could Happen Tomorrow!"

By this time I am walking around in front of my television talking to myself. I am certain you never do this but I did. I was saying to myself, they (that is the secular world) are finally starting to realize that the world as we know it is not going to just keep on going! Things are changing and they are changing fast. It has been my experience through these many years that society in general has a Hollywood view of the world. When I was a boy I remember watching wonderful westerns on TV. I would sit for hours glued to programs watching Roy Rogers, Gene Autry, the Lone Ranger, and a score of others fighting the bad guys and sometimes the Indians. (Oops — can I say that in our politically correct world without offending my Native American friends?) I remember scenes where the Indians would be chasing the good guys who were riding on their white horses. The good guys would always outrun the Indians. In fact, I cannot remember a single time when the Indians caught up with the guy on the white horse. He always got away! This led me to believe for several years as a little boy that white horses were just faster than black or brown ones. Anyway, this hero just kept riding and riding and riding until the Indians finally gave up. The fact is, this is not reality! The truth is that in the real world the good guy was riding and riding and his horse got tired and eventually collapsed. The Indians caught up to the good guy and killed him! Hollywood sells fantasy and Americans buy into it as though it were reality.

Could it be that someone at the Weather Channel was tapping into reality? Is it possible that someone — maybe a producer or director of programming — was a believer? Could it be that someone had perhaps read the Bible and as a result was beginning to understand the seriousness of the world situation? I wanted to know more about this so I went to the Internet and pulled up the Weather Channel's website. I was surprised to find there was a host of weather-related events they were advertising as part of what would be an ongoing series. The thrust was the unexpected weather-related events and the shocking, life-altering impact they could make on society in a matter of seconds.

Finally, I thought to myself, *the world is waking up!* You see, as a preacher and teacher of Bible prophecy I have been saying for years we are living in the end times. I have been heralding a message of the soon return of Jesus Christ everywhere I go. I have spent hundreds if not thousands of hours studying and speaking on this incredible subject, yet the vast majority of people today are simply too busy to pay attention to what is happening around them! We are asleep. Could we be waking up? I truly pray it is so.

I can say with reasonable certainty that long ago when Noah began to build the ark, no one paid any attention to him. Why should they? It had never rained upon the earth. The populace at that time had no idea what rain was and how it could affect their day-to-day lives. No doubt Noah verbally warned his neighbors that something dreadful was going to happen soon. However, then as now, it appears the warning fell on deaf ears. No doubt, Noah was called a prophet of doom. I feel certain people saw him as a negative individual who was not much fun to be around. Yet he was right! God had told him that He, that is God, was going to destroy every living creature on the earth except those inside the ark. (See Genesis 69 for a full explanation.) To the surprise of Noah's world, one day a drop of water fell from the sky, and then another and another. Then a spring burst forth from below the earth. People were shocked! Nothing like this had ever happened before. (The earth before the worldwide Flood existed with a terrarium-like effect. See *The Genesis Record* by Dr. Henry Morris for a complete explanation). Water began to fall in greater amounts. The ground became saturated as the water level continued to rise. Finally, people began fleeing to higher and higher ground but to no avail. The waters continued to rise until there was no place left to run. The entire population of the earth, as well as all the animals, perished. The only survivors were inside the ark! What was the difference between those who lived and those who perished? Answer: Eight people listened and heeded God's warning. Untold thousands paid no attention! In fact the Bible says, "As it was in the days of Noah, so it will be at the coming of the Son of Man. For in the days before the flood, people were eating and drinking, marrying and giving in marriage, up to the day Noah entered the ark; and they knew nothing about what would happen until the flood came and took them all away. That is how it will be at the coming of the Son of man" (Matthew 24:37–39).

Fast forward a few thousand years to our day. The prophetic word of God, found only in the sacred Scriptures, warns us regarding the condition of our world in the last days. Christ Himself tells us of impending wars, rumors of wars, ethnic conflicts, spiritual deception, famines, pestilences, and earthquakes in various places. Jesus said these things would be signs to us that we are in the last days, and yet most are ignoring the warnings that have been given.

That's what this book is about. It is a book of warnings! I believe with all my soul God wants us to be prepared for the disasters that are taking place and those that will come in the near future. This book is about future events that will shake the world — events prophesied long ago by God's ancient prophets and Jesus Himself. Events we should be watching for as well as events that will happen after God's children are gone. Events that are as certain to take place as the sun is to rise in the east and set in the west. I know I will be misunderstood by some, considered a prophet of doom by others, and largely ignored by most. That is okay. I must be true to my own soul and warn as many as possible of the lateness of the hour. Time is running out! As one long-running daytime soap says, "As the sand is through the hourglass, so are the days of our lives!"

That said, this is not a book of doom and gloom. Rather it is a message of hope! In fact, I believe the only ones alive today who have a message of hope for tomorrow are those who know Jesus Christ as Lord of their lives and His Word! Read on and be challenged with hope for the future.

Chapter 1

THE GREAT DISAPPEARING

Ashley laid her six-month-old baby girl, Madison, in her crib, quietly turned out the light and paused at the door for one last glimpse before returning to the living room. Ashley and her husband, Bill, relaxed on the sofa and began to talk about the events of their day. Suddenly, for some strange reason, Ashley jumped from the sofa and immediately bolted to Madison's bedroom and opened the door. She stood in the doorway with disbelief in her eyes. The crib was empty and Madison was gone. It happened just that fast, in the blink of an eye. This same scene played out over and over again in untold thousands of homes in America and throughout the world. One can only imagine the thoughts racing through the hearts and minds of those who found loved ones gone or instantaneously vanish before their eyes. How will people respond? What will they think? Where will they turn? How would you respond and, more important, would you be ready?

What do you suppose would happen if 100 million people vanished from this planet? One can only imagine the terror that would result in such a catastrophic occurrence. Will those who find themselves left behind notice that millions of people were missing. How will it be explained, and by who? Where did they go? Who took them? Why didn't they take me? These are very logical questions, in light of what would have taken place. There is no doubt in my mind that when this worldwide event occurs, the media will be racing to offer one suggestion after another. I can picture reporters standing in the middle of the street attempting to be heard over the screaming of those whose loved ones have simply vanished. No doubt, the networks will feature 24-hour coverage of this incredible event. I can just imagine some of the ideas that will be discussed at news desks around the world. Some will say there has been an abduction by aliens or "space brothers" of all those who needed to undergo evolutionary reprogramming. Others will no doubt speak about the fact that we have long believed that there is life on other planets and now an invasion has finally taken place. But wait a minute. I'm getting ahead of myself. Allow me go back to the beginning, where the story really starts. Let's go back to creation.

Back to the Beginning

God had a plan when He created the galaxies, put the stars and the planets in their place, and created the animals, and lastly, humanity. Scripture clearly says that God already knew the beginning from the end, and that He has had a plan for the earth we occupy since before its creation. Revelation 13:8 says, "All inhabitants of the earth will worship the beast — all whose names have not been written in the book of life belonging to the Lamb that was slain from the creation of the world." Even the crucifixion of Christ was a part of God's plan before there was ever a need for His sacrifice. The Bible is our guide to that plan, and in it we can find a clear, accurate, and reliable picture of what has been and what is yet to come in our world's future.

I personally believe that God's plan is a 7,000-year plan. I realize we are told by the academic world that the earth upon which we reside is millions of years old. In fact, if you visit the Grand Canyon and read the literature provided at the visitor's center, you will be told it was formed 270 million years ago. Was anyone there to substantiate this? Is this fact? I do not concur with the theory of evolution. I know it's hard to read the Bible and at the same time go through our public education system, where you'll be taught this unfounded theory as though it were fact. I might remind those who believe in evolution that even the founder of the theory of evolution, Charles Darwin, admitted that evolution was only a theory. A theory is something that hasn't been proven in an observable, verifiable way. No one has ever seen a monkey evolve into a human. A fish has never been seen sprouting legs and walking out of a body of water onto dry land. Therefore, to teach or accept a theory as fact is academic deception, and believing it takes a giant leap of faith. Since this is true, why not simply accept the creation record in Genesis as being fact? Frankly, I am persuaded it takes a greater step of faith to accept evolution than to simply accept the biblical record.

As I stated, God's plan is a 7,000-year program. From creation to the call of Abraham was two thousand years. From Abraham to Jesus Christ was another two thousand years. From Jesus Christ to the end of the era in which we now live is going to be two thousand years, and then all that's left is the return of Christ and His one-thousand-year reign on earth. I believe this because I believe God is organized. He does not work randomly, as we can see in nature itself. Right now, you might be asking yourself, *How he can say that the time from Christ's sacrifice to His return will be two thousand years when we have already passed the year A.D. 2000?* The fact is, we know that our calendars are not accurate. Your calendar may tell you it's been more than 2,000 years since the time of Christ, but its accuracy was in question from the time it was created. When the sixth-century scholar Dionysius Exiguus created the Gregorian calendar that we use today, he based it on the birth of Christ and the beginning of the Christian era. However, he didn't use an accurate date for the birth of Christ. Since his starting point wasn't accurate, we already know that the year 2000 wasn't really 2,000 years from the time of Christ. That's just one error among many.

We can see evidence of God's ordered, 7,000-year plan when we look at how God works. He created all that exists in six, literal 24-hour days, and rested on the seventh. God initiated seven Jewish feast days, and seven is God's number of perfection. This by itself would not be very good evidence, except that in the New Testament the Apostle Peter states, "But do not forget this one thing, dear friends: With the Lord a day is like a thousand years, and a thousand years are like a day" (2 Peter 3:8).

As I write these words, I am keenly aware that much of modern Christianity and the entire secular academic world dismiss this thought as foolishness. However, this makes perfect sense to me, and as I look at the big picture of God's plan, it fits perfectly with the prophetic teaching of God's Word. I believe it will make perfect sense to you as well, when you've read what God's plan holds in store for us next, and see the convincing proof that exists for our generation being the final generation that will see Christ's return.

- The Bible begins with God creating the world we now live in. He created Adam and Eve, and placed them in a controlled environment with virtually everything they could possibly need or even want. He only placed one restriction on their lives in the Garden of Eden. They were not to eat the fruit from the tree of knowledge of good and evil. Adam and Eve chose to break this command, and sin entered into the world. Over a process of time, as the earth was populated and sin continued to corrupt the lives of the people, God's plan called for the destruction of the world with a global Flood, sparing only eight people — Noah and his family. Following the Flood, these eight people began to repopulate the earth. Once again man's sinful nature led to the continued violation of God's plan of obedience for humankind.

Eventually, God spoke to a man named Abraham, and through Abraham and his wife, Sarah, God miraculously brought a child into the world named Isaac. Thus began the Jewish race upon the earth. The Jews were God's chosen people in a wicked world, and it would be this race that God would use to send a living sacrifice, capable of covering the sins of the world. Jesus, born to a virgin girl named Mary in a small village in Israel called Nazareth, lived upon the earth for 33½ years and was crucified upon a Cross. Three days later He rose from the dead, walked among the people of this earth, and was witnessed by as many as 500 people at one given time before ascending into heaven from the Mount of Olives in Jerusalem. Fifty days after His Resurrection, Christ's Church was born on the Jewish festival of Pentecost, when the followers of Christ received the Holy Spirit, as had been promised by Jesus before His death and Resurrection. Pentecost began the world's final two-thousand-year period, before God's plan will be concluded with the physical reign of Christ upon the earth, known as the Millennial Reign. This period in which we now live will draw to its end in an event known as the Rapture, when Christ will receive unto Himself every person on this globe that has trusted Him as the Savior of his or her soul and the Lord of his or her life.

Jesus described His return and the gathering of the Church in Matthew 24:40–41, when He said, "Two men will be in the field; one will be taken and the other left. Two women will be grinding with a hand mill; one will be taken and the other left."

No matter how hard we try, I don't believe it's possible for anyone to comprehend what this earthshaking event will really be like. Perhaps it's this wonder and mystery that makes the Rapture such a controversial topic in our world today. There is much disagreement, even within the Christian community, regarding the Rapture, and the secular world mocks those who find hope in Christ's promised return for His followers. However, needlessly divisive arguments among Christians, and the opinions of those who don't know any better, make Christ's promise no less real and imminent, as we will see.

What Exactly Is the Rapture, Anyway?

According to the manufacturers of Ping golf clubs, it is the newest and best driver on the market, the Rapture 460. However, this is not the Rapture we are seeking to define in this context. The word "Rapture" comes from a Latin word which has its root in a Greek word meaning to catch up or snatch up. Therefore, when one speaks of the Rapture, one is speaking of an event in which

Jesus Christ will appear in the sky to snatch all true believers up to Himself, and ultimately to heaven.

Many today say that the very idea of the Rapture is traceable only back to the 1860s when a preacher by the name of John Nelson Darby (1800–1882) began to spread this idea among his followers. The Rapture skeptics also point to a young Scottish girl by the name of Margaret McDonald who supposedly had a vision and, from that vision, the idea of a Rapture taking place before the Tribulation period was born. Further, they point out that the word *Rapture* never appears in Scripture. If you point out that the Bible was written in Koine Greek, and not English, they will respond only with a blank stare. It never occurs to them that an English word would be decidedly out of place in Greek writings, and they don't bother to examine what the Bible does say about this prophetic event.

All of these arguments are nothing more than smoke and mirrors. The biblical teaching of the Rapture comes from the Lord Jesus Himself, as well as from the written word of the Apostles. Jesus said to the disciples, as recorded in John 14:1–3, "Do not let your hearts be troubled. Trust in God; trust also in me. In my Father's house are many rooms; if it were not so, I would have told you. And if I go and prepare a place for you, I will come back and take you to be with me that you also may be where I am."

The fact is, Jesus was speaking to those who, by faith, committed themselves to Him. In other words, this earthshaking event is not for everyone, but only for those who love Christ and are looking for His return. The disciples and the early followers of Christ expected Jesus to return in their lifetime. I believe, based on the writings of the Apostles Paul, Peter, and James, that the Bible teaches an eminent return of Christ for His Church.

Since Jesus might come again for His followers at any moment, we must be ready for His return at all times. In addition, I believe His return will precede a seven-year, worldwide tribulation, when God finally judges the wicked nations of the world and those who rejected Christ.

This teaching is commonly known in Christian circles as the Pre-Tribulation view of the Rapture. Is it a new idea? No. However, it is a rediscovered teaching that was lost to the Church for hundreds of years as the world languished through what is labeled historically as the Dark Ages. In the thousand-plus years of the Dark Ages, most could not read, and illiteracy reigned. The Bibles that existed were found mostly in churches, chained to lecterns, and read only by the clergy. In addition, government-controlled religion was the order of the day, and what Scripture the masses did hear was often chosen with politics, money, and power in mind, rather than the spiritual growth of the Church. The result was that some of the great truths of God's prophetic Word were lost to most, and remained so until the period known as the Enlightenment to the secular world, and the Reformation to the Christian world.

The idea that someone might be translated from earth directly into heaven without seeing death is also not a new idea. In the Old Testament, Enoch was taken into the presence of God while still very much alive (Genesis 5:18–24). Hebrews 11:5 tells us that, just as will be the case with the Rapture, faith was a requirement for Enoch to be translated into the presence of the Lord. Likewise, Elijah was taken up into heaven like a whirlwind because of his faith, and was seen no more (2 Kings 2:11–12).

So we can see that the translation of a living human on earth into the heavenly realm has been used by God in the past to bring believers into His presence, but what about the translation of the entire body of believers, prior to the Tribulation? It is a fact that the early Christians looked forward with hope and longing to a time when Christ, as He promised in Matthew 24, would return and translate all believers into the heavenly realm to be with Him in His Father's house. Paul said in 1 Corinthians 15:51–52, "Listen, I tell you a mystery: We will not all sleep, but we will all be changed — in a flash, in the twinkling of an eye, at the last trumpet. For the trumpet will sound, the dead will be raised imperishable, and we will be changed."

THE 15 DIFFERENCES BETWEEN THE

Rapture/Blessed Hope

1. Christ comes in the air for His own
2. Rapture/translation of all Christians
3. Christians are taken to the Father's house
4. No judgment on earth at the Rapture
5. The Church is taken to heaven at Rapture
6. The Rapture is imminent
7. No signs for Rapture
8. For believers only
9. Time of joy
10. Comes before the day of wrath
11. No mention of Satan
12. The Judgment Seat of Christ
13. Marriage of the Lamb
14. Only His own see Him
15. The Tribulation begins

RAPTURE AND THE GLORIOUS APPEARING

Glorious Appearing

1. Christ comes with His own to earth
2. No one is translated
3. Resurrected saints do not see Father's house
4. Christ judges inhabitants of the earth
5. Christ sets up His Kingdom on the earth
6. Can't occur for at least seven years
7. Many signs for Christ's physical coming
8. Affects all mankind
9. Time of mourning
10. Immediately after Tribulation
11. Satan bound/bottomless pit for 1,000 years
12. No time or place for Judgment Seat
13. His Bride descends with Him
14. Every eye shall see Him
15. 1,000-year Kingdom of Christ begins

A Biblical View of the Rapture

It should be enough that the Bible clearly teaches a Pre-Tribulation Rapture, but for those who need more than the perfect Word of God to convince them, there are a number of historical sources that prove a much earlier belief in the eminent return of Christ and a Pre-Tribulation Rapture, than skeptics would lead us to believe. One of these sources is the Pseudo-Ephraem sermon, written by the Syrian, Ephraem in A.D. 372.[1] Three historical references state that this sermon was written by Ephraem, and several scholars have concluded that, whether it was written by Ephraem in the fourth century, or later, it was clearly written before the sixth century — over 1,000 years before Darby concluded that a complete Rapture of the Church would occur before the tribulation.

In section 2 of Ephraem's sermon, he wrote of the end times, saying, ". . . and there is no other which remains, except the advent of the wicked one in the completion of the Roman kingdom. Why therefore are we occupied with worldly business, and why is our mind held fixed on the lusts of the world or on the anxieties of the ages? Why therefore do we not reject every care of worldly business, and why is our mind held fixed on the lusts of the world or on the anxieties of the ages? Why therefore do we not reject every care of earthly actions and prepare ourselves for the meeting of the Lord Christ, so that he may draw us from the confusion, which overwhelms all the world?" Later in Section 2 he continues, "For all the saints and elect of God are gathered, prior to the tribulation that is to come, and are taken to the Lord lest they see the confusion that is to overwhelm the world because of our sins." Obviously, this agrees with the Pre-Tribulation view of the Rapture. We need not concern ourselves with stockpiling food, preparing for war and destruction, or the worries of the world during the end times, because we will be spared God's judgment on the wicked.

Ephraem goes on to say in section 4, "Because those very much horrible nations, most profane and most defiled, who do not spare

---

1. http://www.biblefacts.org/church/ephream.html.

lives, and shall destroy the living from the dead, shall consume the dead, they eat dead flesh, they drink the blood of beasts, they pollute the world, contaminate all things, and the one who is able to resist them is not there."

It's clear that this sermon from the fourth century taught the same Pre-Tribulation view of the event we call the Rapture well before the Reformation, when this doctrine was restored, and long before Darby came to the same conclusion.

There are also later historical sources that predate Darby's teachings. Morgan Edwards, a well-respected pastor of the Baptist Church in Philadelphia during the 1760s and the premier Baptist historian of his day, is just one of them. He published his seminal works, "Millennium" and "Last Novelties," in 1881, which contained some of his writings from the early 1740s. His earlier writings indicate that, while Edwards believed in a Rapture of the Church at the midpoint in the Tribulation, he clearly interpreted Scripture to say that believers would be spared from wrath and would be snatched away to face judgment at the Bema seat in heaven before Christ returns to establish his millennial kingdom. Like Pre-Tribulationists, he saw Christ's return for His Church as a separate event from His return at the end of the Tribulation.

I've shown that the belief in a Pre-Tribulation Rapture of the saints is not a new idea cooked up by heretics in the 1800s, but let's look in depth at the most important source of truth we have. The very Word of God clearly tells us that Christ will return for His Church before the rise of Antichrist and the beginning of the seven-year Tribulation.

The Difference between the Rapture and the Second Coming

The first thing we need to understand is the difference between the Rapture and the Second Coming of Christ. When Christ returns before the Tribulation, He will come to gather the saints, both the living and the dead, and they will join Him in the clouds. All believers will be taken to be with Christ in His Father's house in heaven. However, when Christ returns at the end of the Tribulation, He will come with all power and glory to bind Satan and defeat the wicked nations of the earth, the Antichrist, and the False Prophet. Most importantly, when Christ returns following the Tribulation, the Saints will already be with Him!

Let's look at the difference in Scripture. First Thessalonians 4:16–18 says, "For the Lord himself will come down from heaven, with a loud command, with the voice of the archangel and with the trumpet call of God, and the dead in Christ will rise first. After that, we who are still alive and are left will be caught up together with them in the clouds to meet the Lord in the air. And so we will be with the Lord forever. Therefore encourage each other with these words." Notice that in this verse believers will be caught up in the air and will be taken to be "with" Christ in His Father's house. Now, consider Matthew 24:30–31 which reads, "At that time the sign of the Son of Man will appear in the sky, and all the nations of the earth will mourn. They will see the Son of Man coming on the clouds of the sky, with power and great glory. And he will send his angels with a loud trumpet call, and they will gather his elect from the four winds, from one end of the heavens to the other." In this verse, when Christ returns to judge the nations after the Tribulation, believers are gathered from one end of the heavens to the other. In other words, when Christ returns to defeat Satan, the Church will already be in heaven.

Another example can be found in John 14:1–4. Here, Jesus comforts believers by telling them, "Do not let your hearts be troubled. Trust in God; trust also in me. In my Father's house are many rooms; if it were not so, I would have told you. I am going there to prepare a place for you. And if I go and prepare a place for you, I will come back and take you to be with me that you also may be where I am." Once again, Jesus promises to return and take believers to be with Him in heaven. However, in Revelation we read about a very different event at the Tribulation's end.

I saw heaven standing open and there before me was a white horse, whose rider is called Faithful and True. With justice he judges and makes war. His eyes are like blazing fire, and on his head are many crowns. He has a name written on him that no one knows but he himself. He is dressed in a robe dipped in blood, and his name is the Word of God. The armies of heaven were following him, riding on white horses and dressed in fine linen, white and clean. Out of his mouth comes a sharp sword with which to strike down the nations (Revelation 19:11–15).

In these verses, as Christ returns at the end of the Tribulation to defeat the Antichrist and his followers, the Saints return with Him. They are not being gathered to Him and taken into heaven, as with the Rapture passages. Proponents of the Post-Tribulation view will argue that the Church still could have been caught up in the air after the Tribulation, and just prior to Christ's return, only to turn around and come right back down for the final battle between good and evil. However, we've already seen that the saints are gathered from the corners of heaven, and not from the earth below, before the glorious appearing of Christ.

Chapter 19 of John's Revelation provides even further proof that we are indeed in heaven before the glorious appearing. At the beginning of chapter 19, you'll find a description of the Marriage Supper of the Lamb. Verse seven says that the Bride of Christ (the Church) has made herself ready, and we read of great rejoicing and preparation in heaven for the glorious appearing. If the marriage supper of the Lamb happens before the glorious appearing, then the Church must be present in heaven. What is a marriage supper without the bride?!

We're also told in Revelation 19:8 that believers are made ready for the marriage supper by their righteous acts. Since it is the judgment seat of Christ where these righteous acts (or lack thereof, as the case may be) are judged, the judgment of believers must also take place after the Rapture, while the Church is in heaven. This is further demonstrated in Ephesians 5:27, which describes the Bride of Christ (the Church) being presented to the bridegroom at the marriage supper of the Lamb without stain or wrinkle, or any other blemish, but holy and blameless. Since believers will only exist in this state after the bema seat judgment (the final judgment for believers), when the Church has been cleansed and made whole, we must conclude that the final judgment for believers takes place in heaven before the marriage supper of the Lamb. As we learned earlier, the marriage supper comes before Christ returns to defeat the Antichrist and issue final judgment on those who followed him during the Tribulation. Believers can't be on earth with those who are suffering through the Tribulation and the rule of the Antichrist, and be in heaven being judged for their works by Christ at the same time. The fact is, they were raptured seven years earlier and have been resting in the rooms Jesus went to prepare for them, when they are gathered together for these final events before the glorious appearing of Christ.

As these verses show, Christ gathers His Church to be with Him in heaven before the tribulation begins, and those same believers return with Him for the final battle at the end of the Antichrist's seven-year reign. But we need not depend only on these verses for scriptural proof.

Now that we understand the difference between the Rapture and the glorious appearing, let's look deeper into what Scripture has to say about the timing of the Rapture. There are three main views on the Rapture's timing. There are other less widely held views, but they are so lacking in scriptural support as to be not worth mentioning here.

One Rapture theory, the Mid-Tribulation view, holds that believers will be raptured at the midpoint of the tribulation, exactly 3½ years before Christ's glorious appearing. The Post-Tribulation view, on the other hand, sees believers going through the entire Tribulation period on earth, and only when God's judgment on the nations is over, will they meet the Lord in the air at His glorious appearing. They will then turn around and follow Christ right back down for the final battle of Armageddon. There are some slight variations in those beliefs, but that's the gist of it. As you will see, the Pre-Tribulation view is the only view that allows for an imminent, unexpected return of Christ, both of which Scripture tells us are necessary characteristics of the Rapture.

As we examine the timing of the Rapture, you might be surprised to learn that there are actually several verses in the Bible that tell us in no uncertain terms that Christians will not suffer through the Tribulation. So how can anyone believe in a Mid- or Post-Tribulation Rapture if this is true? To that, I can only say, people see what they want to see sometimes. Perhaps guilt over how they've lived their lives causes them to feel they deserve to be judged along with the wicked. Perhaps, as with the Catholic belief in purgatory, they feel they should have to take part in Christ's sacrifice by suffering for some of their sins, even though the Bible tells us we are saved by grace and not by anything we can do. Whatever their reasons, they must ignore a great deal of Scripture to believe that we won't be kept from the wrath of the Tribulation. Take, for example, these words from Paul:

> But you, brothers, are not in darkness so that this day should surprise you like a thief. You are all sons of the light and sons of the day. We do not belong to the night or to the darkness. So then, let us not be like others, who are asleep, but let us be alert and self-controlled. For those who sleep, sleep at night, and those who get drunk, get drunk at night. But since we belong to the day, let us be self-controlled, putting on faith and love as a breastplate, and the hope of salvation as a helmet. For God did not appoint us to suffer wrath but to receive salvation through our Lord Jesus Christ. He died for us so that, whether we are awake or asleep, we may live together with him (1 Thessalonians 5:4–10).

It can't get any more straightforward than that. Followers of Christ are not destined to suffer God's wrath, but to live with the Lord. As we learned earlier in verses 16 through 18, the dead in Christ, along with those who are still alive, will be caught up in the air to be with the Lord in heaven. Verses 9 and 10 reveal the timing of this event. We will be raptured before God pours out his judgment on the nations during the Tribulation.

God felt it was so important for us to know this fact, so that we would not fear His judgment on the world, that He repeated this assurance several times in Scripture. Romans 5:9 says, "Since we have now been justified by his blood, how much more shall we be saved from God's wrath through him!" Paul also said in 1 Thessalonians 1:10 "to wait for his Son from heaven, whom he raised from the dead — Jesus, who rescues us from the coming wrath."

As further evidence of this precious truth, numerous verses indicate the absence of the Church during the Tribulation. For example, 2 Thessalonians 2, verses 3 and 6 through 7, say that the Holy Spirit won't be present on earth during the Tribulation. However, Jesus told us in John 14:16–17, when He promised to send us a counselor and comforter to be with us in His absence, that the Holy Spirit would dwell within the hearts of believers forever. If the Church were on earth during the Tribulation, then it couldn't be said that the Holy Spirit had been taken out of the way. We can reason from this, then, that the Church, along with the Holy Spirit, is removed before the Tribulation begins.

Paul issued a warning to believers in his second letter to the church of the Thessalonians. He said, "Concerning the coming of our Lord Jesus Christ and our being gathered to him, we ask you, brothers, not to become easily unsettled or alarmed by some prophecy, report or letter supposed to have come from us, saying that the day of the Lord has already come. Don't let anyone deceive you in any way, for that day will not come until the rebellion occurs and the man of lawlessness is revealed, the man doomed to destruction" (2 Thessalonians 2:1–3). The word rebellion in this verse comes from the Greek noun *apostasia*, and it is used only twice in the New Testament. One of those instances is found in Acts 21:21 where, speaking of Paul, it says "you teach all the Jews who live among the Gentiles to turn away from (*apostasia*) Moses." *Apostasia* is a Greek compound of *apo*, which means "from," and *istemi*, which means "stand." One of its meanings in the Greek Lexicon is "departure, or disappearance." Interestingly, it is this definition that was used in the first seven English translations of the Bible. In fact, Jerome's A.D. 400 Latin translation of the Bible known as the Vulgate renders *apostasia* with the word *discessio*, meaning "departure." It wasn't until the King James Version of the Bible was written that translators began using the new rendering of "falling away." The earlier translations support the notion that this verse is referring to a Pre-Tribulation Rapture.

We've established that the Holy Spirit will be "taken out of the way" during the Tribulation, allowing the Antichrist to deceive the masses without opposition or any resistance that might serve to restrain him in his pursuit of global rule. In Isaiah, chapter 26, we find yet further evidence that believers were taken out of the way before the Tribulation began.

> But your dead will live; their bodies will rise. You who dwell in the dust, wake up and shout for joy. Your dew is like the dew of the morning; the earth will give birth to her dead. Go, my people, enter your rooms and shut the doors behind you; hide yourselves for a little while until his wrath has passed by. See, the LORD is coming out of his dwelling to punish the people of the earth for their sins. The earth will disclose the blood shed upon her; she will conceal her slain no longer (Isaiah 26:19–21).

It is mind-boggling, really, that anyone could read these verses and not take from it an assurance that God will Rapture His Church before He pours out His wrath and judgment on the world. Remember, Jesus told His followers that after His Resurrection He would be going to prepare a place for us. He promised to return at some later time and take us to be with Him, where we will dwell within the many rooms of His Father's house. These verses from Isaiah tell us that believers will be hidden in these rooms, while God punishes the earth's inhabitants for their sinful, rebellious ways.

A Matter of Common Sense and Logic

There is still one other way we can know with certainty that the Rapture will precede the Tribulation, and it's really a matter of common sense and logic. The Pre-Tribulation view is the only view that allows for the imminent return of Christ. Both the Mid-Tribulation and Post-Tribulation views would make it possible to know exactly when Christ will return. All one would need to do is count either three and a half years, in the case of a Mid-Tribulation Rapture, or seven years in the case of a Post-Tribulation Rapture, from the peace agreement between the Antichrist and Israel, and you would arrive at the date for Christ's return. So what's the problem with knowing the exact timing of Christ's return? The problem is, the Bible tells us that no one knows when Christ will return, not even the angels in heaven. It will be sudden and unexpected by every person on this planet. Consider the following verses and ask yourself why God would tell us to be on guard, always ready and alert, if we could predict when Christ was going to return.

> Therefore keep watch, because you do not know on what day your Lord will come (Matthew 24:42).

> So you also must be ready, because the Son of Man will come at an hour when you do not expect him (Matthew 24:44).

> No one knows about that day or hour, not even the angels in heaven, nor the Son, but only the Father (Matthew 24:36).

> Therefore keep watch, because you do not know the day or the hour (Matthew 25:13).

The answer is, He wouldn't warn us to be alert if He expected us to know when Christ was going to return. The Rapture will come like a "thief in the night," because there is nothing left to be fulfilled before Christ can return for His Church. It could happen tomorrow, and no prophecy would be left unfulfilled. You see, it's only a surprise if we don't need the Antichrist's rise to power and the Tribulation to happen first.

With a Pre-Tribulation view of the Rapture, no one can assume they have around three and a half, or seven years left to get their affairs in order and get right with God before Christ returns. It is the only view that makes sense in light of several verses that warn us to live as if Christ were returning tomorrow.

That is not to say we aren't supposed to watch for the signs of His return. While there are no prophetic events yet to be fulfilled before the Rapture can occur, there are many signs, including the signs Jesus told us to watch for, that indicate this is the generation that will be snatched up to meet the Lord in the air.

There's a reason Christ warned us 13 times in the New Testament to watch for the signs of His return, and be ready. He wanted us to be excited about His return, and be motivated by its imminence to save as many souls as we can in the time we have left. In the chapters ahead I will outline these signs for you, and together we will feel the same hope and assurance that sustained the Apostles and moved first-century believers to spread the good news far and wide, even while suffering horrible persecution for their efforts. As we watch the wicked world around us paving the way for the Antichrist's tyrannical rule, we will be able to look to the clouds with hope, and know that our rooms in heaven, prepared by Jesus Himself, await us.

Oh, by the way, remember Ashley and Bill, Madison's mom and dad? They went to church the next Sunday and listened while the preacher tried to explain away their sorrow. He gave a number of possibilities of what might have happened but nothing he said could fill the void that had been left in their hearts.

Chapter 2

AMERICA IN PROPHECY

On many occasions, I have stood on the bow of a relatively small boat as it sailed across the Sea of Galilee. The captain would come and hoist the American flag as the singing of our National Anthem rose to meet it. During many of these moving, emotional moments, I have pondered in my heart where America would be in the last days, and how the demise of this great country might come about. Movies abound with story lines of the destruction of these United States. Sometimes the story line involves a giant meteor that wipes us off the surface of the earth. Then there is the deadly virus for which there is no cure. Oh, and we dare not forget the Martians, and the multitudes of people who truly believe we are on the verge of an invasion from outer space.

People often ask me why America is absent in Scripture, and what happens to America in the end times. These are two very interesting questions. Simply put, America is never mentioned in Scripture because she did not exist at the time the Bible was written. The canon of Scripture was closed in A.D. 325, some 1,100-plus years before the discovery of America. That said, America has, without question, been the greatest nation on the globe for more than 234 years. The world would be in big trouble without the United States in many arenas. She is the greatest missionary-sending country on the face of the earth and has been the most charitable and hospitable country in the history of the world. She has also been the target of more criticism and envy than all the remaining nations combined. We as Americans are either heroes or enemies, depending on which part of the terra firma one happens to be standing at the moment.

Does America Fit in Bible Prophecy?

I believe America was born of God. No doubt, in the darkness and death of the Spanish Inquisition, God moved in the heart of Christopher Columbus to seek a new land. Peter Marshall, in his best-selling book *The Light and the Glory*, writes of Columbus' personal diary, which states that God led him to discover this new land. A land where there would be freedom to worship or not to worship; a land where the God of heaven would be honored and served as creator of all; a land where individual rights and freedoms would not be taken away.[1] Since her birth, God has blessed this great nation over and over again. In Genesis, God promised to bless those nations who bless Israel, and America is evidence that God keeps His promises. Perhaps it is America's history of successes and great wealth that leads some to believe that America must fit somewhere into end-times prophecy.

Unfortunately, some will try to fit the United States into various Scripture passages, either by taking verses out of context or by ignoring historical and cultural information relevant to the interpretation of that Scripture. This effort is akin to forcing a square peg into a round hole, and only serves to make prophecy confusing when it doesn't need to be. For example, Isaiah 18 speaks of a "tall and smooth" people who come from a powerful nation "whose land the rivers divide." Some have claimed that these people who are "feared far and wide" must be a reference to Americans, because the United States is divided by the Mississippi River and has come to be the most feared nation on the planet, militarily. Both

---

1. Peter Marshall and David Manuel, *The Light and the Glory* (Grand Rapids, MI: Baker House, 1977).

of these statements are true. However, when you put this verse in context, it's clear from verse one that Isaiah was speaking of Cush, or Ethiopia, located on the continent of Africa, and not the United States. In Isaiah's time, Cush was a part of the Egyptian empire, and the river referred to in these verses is the Nile, not the Mississippi.

Ezekiel 38:13 is also sometimes used to claim that America has a role in God's plan for the last days. As we will learn in chapter 4, several nations will launch a diplomatic protest against the Post-Rapture Islamic invasion of Israel. The "merchants of Tarshish and all her villages" are mentioned among those who will protest. Pointing to the fact that Tarshish was the westernmost trading nation in Ezekiel's time, Tarshish becomes Britain because it is the most western point on the continent. From there, they reason, the merchants and villages of Tarshish must be a reference to the former British colonies, which included America before her war for independence was fought and won. This is a real stretch, since the historical evidence, as well as current archaeological evidence, places Tarshish in modern-day Spain.

Another common misinterpretation can be found in Revelation 12:13–17. Here we are told that, during the Tribulation the Jewish remnant will be provided a means of escape, and will be carried away on the wings of an eagle. While it might be tempting to assume the eagle symbolizes America coming to Israel's rescue, the real answer is given to us in the Old Testament. This is a direct comparison to the Exodus explained in Deuteronomy 32. It was the Lord alone who "like an eagle that stirs up its nest and hovers over its young, that spreads its wings to catch them" (Deuteronomy 32:11) led them out of Egypt. It will be God Himself who rescues Israel from her enemies during the Tribulation, not America.

There are many such attempts to insert America into Bible prophecy, but probably one of the most popular theories is one that interprets "Babylon the Great, Mother of Harlots" as being America. Revelation 18:3 refers to a fallen Babylon the great by saying, "For all the nations have drunk the maddening wine of her adulteries. The kings of the earth committed adultery with her, and the merchants of the earth grew rich from her excessive luxuries." At first glance, this does seem to paint a perfect picture of the wealth and moral decline of America. The fact that these Scriptures go on to mention sailors who see the city burning from their ships adds to the temptation to see America in these verses. The tragedy of September 11, 2001, comes to mind, reminding us of the televised scenes of New York and Washington, D.C. As cameras panned across the waters between New York and the island of Manhattan, the Twin Towers could be seen burning with billowing smoke from the opposite shore. This scene was played over and over in the days following 9/11, prompting some Christians to claim it was a fulfillment of prophecy, and America must be the mystery Babylon referred to in the Book of Revelation.

The problem with this interpretation is that, when describing geographical locations, the Bible uses Israel as its point of reference. These verses are describing events from Israel's perspective, not America's. We are also given conclusive proof that America is not Babylon the Great in chapter 17 of Revelation, when John tells us that mystery Babylon is actually a great harlot who will rule the world.

Questions to Answer

If America isn't mentioned in the Bible, then the next logical question is why? There are several possible answers to that question. It could be that America will be a part of the events that will occur before and during the Tribulation, but God simply chose not to mention it. This seems unlikely, especially since Scripture indicates that Europe will be the dominant power in the world during the Tribulation. It's also possible that America is not mentioned specifically because she will be destroyed by her enemies before the Tribulation begins. Another similar possibility is that through moral, spiritual, and economic decline, America will implode from within, allowing a unified Europe to assume America's current position as the world's only superpower during the end times.

We can be certain of one thing, whether America falls due to economic collapse or a military defeat — she will not be a significant power or player in the Antichrist's global system.

Another indication that America will suffer a fall from power of some kind is found in the prophecies that describe the Arab world's willingness and ability to attack Israel just prior to the Tribulation. America is Israel's staunchest defender and ally. Without America's influence and protection, Israel most likely would have been attacked and destroyed long ago. It stands to reason that if the Arab countries, along with Russia, feel confident in their ability to attack and defeat Israel, the threat of American retaliation that now holds them back will most likely no longer exist. Of all the events recorded in Bible prophecy, the most likely verses to mention the existence of America during the Tribulation would be those that depict an attack on America's only ally in the Middle East. We might also expect to find mention of the world's superpower in prophecies describing the signing of a peace treaty between the Antichrist and Israel. Yet, the only countries mentioned during the Antichrist's rise to power are part of a European alliance, with the central headquarters for his global government being in Rome.

It becomes very clear, the more end-time prophecies we examine, that the United States will not be the powerful nation that it is today during the Tribulation. So what could possibly cause the fall of the world's only remaining superpower? There are numerous possibilities that present themselves if we look at the current political, economic, and military climate in the world today.

Enemies of America

America faces many threats from both internal and external sources. The threat of global terrorism was made very real to us with the attacks of September 11, 2001, and the subsequent attacks on Madrid, Britain, and in nearly every country around the world prove that our enemy has the determination and resolve to attack us again. As horrifying as those attacks were, a terrorist with a nuclear weapon could make that destruction, loss of life, and hit to the global economy look small by comparison. Whether our leaders will admit it or not, such an attack on the American homeland is a real possibility. I can guarantee, when the Senate Democrats banned the use of the words "global war on terror"[2] in all future legislation proposed by Democrats, terrorists around the world were laughing. They know we are in a global struggle for our very existence, and as long as politicians are willing to pretend that the terrorist threat isn't real, another attack is inevitable.

A future attack that could bring America to her knees might come from one of many threats. It's been known for some time that Russia is providing Iran with the means to acquire nuclear weapons.[3] Iranian President Mahmoud Ahmadinejad has vowed time after time that Iran will never surrender to the West's demands to suspend its nuclear program, and stop enriching Uranium. In response to toothless U.N. resolutions ordering the cessation of all nuclear activity, Ahmadinejad has responded with bellicose rants promising the annihilation of Israel, and the death of America.[4] He continues to insist that Iran has a right to benefit from nuclear technology and power, even though Iran's enormous oil reserves make reliance on nuclear power unnecessary. In one of his latest rampages he stated, "Nothing will stop his nation from pursuing nuclear capabilities. [Iranians] will not back down one iota in defense of their rights. . . . The nuclear issue was the most important challenge since the revolution but with the help of God and your resistance, it is ending in favor of the Iranian nation."[5]

Making Ahmadinejad's threats even more ominous is his obsession with the return of the 12th Imam or Mahdi. He believes,

2. Scott Wilson and Al Kamen, " 'Global War On Terror' Is Given New Name," *The Washington Post*, March 25, 2009, p. A04.

3. Victor Mizin, "The RussiaIran Nuclear Connection and U.S. Policy Options," *Middle East Review of International Affairs (MERIA)*, volume 8, no. 1 March 2004, http://meria.idc.ac.il/ journal/2004/issue1/jv8n1a7.html.

4. "Ahmadinejad to Iranians: Israel 'will be removed,' " worldnetdaily.com, February 20, 2006, http://www.wnd. com/news/article.asp?ARTICLE_ID=48790.

5. hftm.org/blog/?p=323.

as he's described candidly in several interviews and speeches, that he is destined to play a significant role in the appearance of the Mahdi in the end times.[6] Every move he makes, every speech, and every threat is an attempt to hasten the Mahdi's return and the judgment that Muslims believe will befall the enemies of Islam in the end times.

Ahmadinejad's preoccupation with the Mahdi is raising concerns in the West that a nuclear Iran could actually bring about the global war that he envisions taking place upon the Mahdi's arrival.

In a videotaped meeting with Ayatollah Javadi Amoli in Tehran, Ahmadinejad described an event that took place while he was addressing the United Nations in New York in 2006. He recounted being surrounded by a green light from heaven that supposedly shone down on the podium. A transcript of the speech indicates that others from his entourage alerted him to the light, which, they say, appeared as he spoke the words "in the name of Allah." Ahmadinejad also claims that for the 28 minutes he spoke, none of the world leaders in the audience blinked. To him, and those in his delegation, it was taken as a clear sign that Ahmadinejad's main mission is to pave the path for the reappearance of Imam Mahdi. He has said as much in several speeches, including a speech in Tehran on November 16, 2006.[7]

Interestingly, Muslims believe that when the Mahdi returns, he will reign on earth for seven years, before bringing about a final judgment, and the end of the world.[8] Muhammad, who lived 500-plus years after the final books of the Bible were written, was very good at plagiarizing parts of the Bible, while changing the meaning to cast Islam as the true religion and the final victor in the battle between good and evil.

Nuclear weapons in the hands of a man who sees himself as the Mahdi's "John the Baptist," and has a long history of funding and

---

6. "Iran Prepares People for 'Messiah Miracles,' " Worldnetdaily.com, January 27, 2007, http//www.worldnetdaily.com/ news/article.asp?ARTICLE_ID=53964.

7. Ibid.

8. "Imam Mahdi, The 12th Imam," http://www.inplainsite.org/html/imam_mahdi.html.

arming terrorists around the world, poses a very real and dangerous threat to the United States. A nuclear weapon detonated by Islamic terrorists in Washington D.C. or other major cities in the United States could kill millions, and destroy the U.S. economy, our way of life, and our status as the world's superpower.

Unfortunately, the nuclear threat of the Cold War and decades of dodging the bullet have left Americans and our leaders with a false sense of security. Political correctness in government and the media have left the American people completely ignorant of the true nature of the enemy we face. The nuclear threat in Iran is much different from the nuclear standoffs of old where Russian and American nuclear warheads were each aimed at the other's major cities. We can no longer rely on the threat of mutually assured destruction. Why? Because, we're dealing with an enemy that thinks we would be doing them a favor by killing them and giving them a free pass to heaven. The threat of massive military retaliation in response to a nuclear attack by Iran, or the terrorists they support, is seen by Iran's leaders as an incentive, not a deterrent, and judging by the national pride displayed as throngs of cheering Iranians take to the streets whenever Ahmadinejad makes announcements on the progress of their nuclear program, it seems foolish to count on a public backlash to quell Ahmadinejad's zeal. Throughout the crowd of hundreds of thousands of Iranians, signs can be seen hoisted in the air with slogans like "nuclear energy is our natural right," and "death to America."[9] While Iran surely has its moderates who see America as an opportunity rather than an enemy, the apocalyptic mood of Ahmadinejad and those who support him makes the threat from Iran's nuclear program a serious one that we ignore at our own peril.

The detonation of a nuclear weapon in a major city is not the only nuclear threat facing America. In fact, there is a far more likely nuclear scenario that, unfortunately, is too often ignored by those

---

9. "Ahmadinejad: We'll Never Give Up Nuclear Program," *Jerusalem Post*, February 11, 2008, http://www.jpost.com.

who plan for future threats. A nuclear weapon detonated above the earth's surface at altitudes between 25 and 250 miles (40–400 km) would cause far greater damage, and affect a much wider area than a nuclear weapon detonated on the ground. The mid-air detonation would interact with the Earth's atmosphere, ionosphere, and magnetic field to produce an electromagnetic pulse, or EMP. In addition to any destruction the blast might cause, the EMP would impact all electrical systems across a wide geographical area. How wide? A nuclear weapon detonated at an altitude of 250 miles over the central United States would cover, with its primary electromagnetic pulse, the entire country of the United States and parts of Canada and Mexico![10] One EMP could send the United States back to the 19th century by knocking out all power to our already-stressed electrical grid, all telecommunications and transportation, banking and financial systems, and all computers in homes, businesses, and government buildings across the country. The effects would be far-reaching, affecting access to fuel, which is pumped using electricity, emergency services, water treatment facilities, and the delivery of food, medication, medical supplies, and a host of other items essential to life. The shipment of consumer goods would come to a screeching halt, and what remained in stores would spoil as refrigeration went out. Spoiling food, the inability to sanitize and distribute water, and the inevitable fires that would rage out of control would threaten public health, and leave hospitals helpless to respond. In addition to these direct effects, lawlessness would take hold in cities across the country. We saw with hurricane Katrina the kind of chaos and confusion that can break out when society is faced with catastrophic damage and the disruption of normal services.

According to Jon Kyl, who chairs the Senate Subcommittee on Terrorism, Technology, and Homeland security, an EMP attack is probably the easiest way for our enemies, terrorist or otherwise, to

---

10. "Our Nation at Risk — the Threat of EMP," Chuck Missler, July 27, 2006, Koinonia House Online, http://www.khouse.org/articles/2005/585.

defeat the United States.[11] It's also important to note that an EMP can be generated without the use of a nuclear weapon. While the information is still classified, it is known that the United States does its EMP research at Kirtland Air Force Base in New Mexico, and it involves the use of high-power microwaves. Weaponized high-powered microwaves can be generated by a device known as a vircator, according to Australian research, and would be far easier for a terrorist to fit inside compact explosives or conventional weapons, which are more readily available and easier to deploy.

The threat of an EMP attack is not a new one; it's simply a more plausible scenario in today's climate of terrorism and Islamic fundamentalism than it has been in the past. Both China and Russia are capable of executing an EMP attack, and have actually made veiled threats in the past. During the NATO led strike on Yugoslavia in 1999, high-ranking members of the Russian Duma alluded to an EMP attack that could destroy the United States.[12] In addition, Russia has been all too willing to sell Iran the necessary equipment for their nuclear program, so there's no reason to believe EMP technology wouldn't be on the table as well.

It is countries like Iran and North Korea that many experts believe pose the biggest threat to the United States, either from a direct attack by either country or the detonation of an EMP that finds its way into terrorist hands. Whether it's a rogue state, or one of Iran's many terrorist allies, one EMP could send America back to the stone ages and permanently end her days as the world's leader in anything.

It's a fact that Iran wouldn't hesitate to act out either of these scenarios. They continue to defy the world and expand their uranium enrichment program in the face of near unanimous world condemnation, and they aggressively support terrorism in Iraq, the Palestinian territories, and Afghanistan. However, they aren't counting on weapons of mass destruction as their only means for

---

11. Ibid.
12. Ibid.

bringing about the death of America. A possibly even greater and more eminent threat lies in our dependence on foreign oil sales to keep the dollar and the U.S. economy strong.

The dollar has long been the reserve currency of the world. The United States has maintained that status, even though the dollar ceased to be backed by gold in the '70s, by ensuring that the dollar remains the currency used by most of the world for the purchase of oil. In essence, foreign reserves of U.S. dollars became backed by oil instead of gold. Because 68 percent of all oil is purchased with U.S. dollars through exchanges in the United States and the United Kingdom, foreign governments are forced to maintain a reserve of U.S. dollars in order to facilitate their oil purchases.[13] This stockpiling of the dollar ensures that the dollar remains strong.

Iran understands this concept, and in 2006 they began a project to create the Iranian Oil Bourse (exchange). The Iranian exchange now allows Iran, the second largest oil producer in the world, to trade petrochemicals, crude oil, and oil and gas products in euros or other currencies such as the Japanese yen or the Chinese yuan or renminbi instead of dollars. Nations will no longer be forced to buy and hold dollars in order to secure their payment for oil products, and will instead be able to make oil transactions using their own currencies. This will give the euro a reserve status, thereby strengthening the European economy and dealing a devastating blow to the strength of the dollar and the United States economy.[14]

Countries like China and Japan will benefit by being able to diversify with euros, thus eliminating their economies' dependence on the strength of the dollar and protecting them from its depreciation. As countries around the world dump dollars in exchange for euros or, better yet, gold in order to purchase oil, Americans will see a steep rise in inflation. Most economists predict it will have a severe negative impact on the American economy. Some have gone so far

13. Niusha Boghrati, "Iran's Oil Bourse: A Threat to the US Economy?" worldpress. org, April 11, 2006, http://www.worldpress.org/Mideast/2314.cfm.
14. Krassimir Petrov, "The Proposed Iranian Oil Bourse," *Energy Bulletin*, January 17, 2006, http://www.energybulletin.net/print.php?id=12125.

as to predict the worst economic disaster to hit the states since the Great Depression, possibly making it impossible for America to import goods because of the severe devaluation of the dollar.[15]

I should also point out that recently Japan, China, Russia, and France met to discuss a new world currency called the bancor to replace the dollar as the new world currency. Note the following article:

> **June 29, 2010 New York (CNN)** — The dollar is an unreliable international currency and should be replaced by a more stable system, the United Nations Department of Economic and Social Affairs said in a report released Tuesday.
>
> The use of the dollar for international trade came under increasing scrutiny when the U.S. economy fell into recession. "The dollar has proved not to be a stable store of value, which is a requisite for a stable reserve currency," the report said.
>
> Many countries, in Asia in particular, have been building up massive dollar reserves. As a result, those countries' currencies have become undervalued, decreasing their ability to import goods from abroad.
>
> The World Economic and Social Survey 2010 is supporting a proposal long advocated by the International Monetary Fund to create a standardized international system for liquidity transfer.
>
> Under this proposed system, countries would no longer have to buy up foreign currencies, as China has long done with the U.S. dollar. Rather, they would accumulate the right to claim foreign currencies, or special drawing rights, or SDRs, rather than the currencies themselves.
>
> The special drawing rights would be backed by a basket of currencies, which would make them less susceptible to volatility in any one currency. And because the value of a

15. Ibid.

special drawing right is defined by the IMF, changes in the value of any one currency could be adjusted for.

America has many enemies around the world who harbor resentment toward the most successful nation on the planet, whether for religious or political reasons, or in many cases jealousy. They would see this new exchange as an opportunity to wrest control of OPEC from the Americans, and would relish the idea of America becoming a Third World country overnight. This scenario would also fit perfectly into end-times prophecy, as Europe stands to gain the most power and influence from Iran's acceptance of payment in Euros and other currencies.

America faces many threats that could bring about her destruction and shift the balance of power to Europe. However, it's entirely possible that an outside influence won't be the catalyst that propels America into chaos, and shatters her economy and political influence. The internal ramifications of the Rapture alone could bring about this shift in power, and force America to look to Europe for her needs and her security. Remember, the Rapture will change everything, and no country will be harder hit than the United States. Without question, there are more Christians in America than in any other nation on earth. While there are still many Christians in Europe, it's becoming an increasingly godless society. Even the mere mention of Europe's Christian heritage was banned from being included in the E.U. constitution.[16] In many areas, there is a palpable hostility toward Christianity, which is only heightened by the growing Muslim population in many European countries. There are still small communities of Christians in Europe, but the vast majority of the population have bought into the secularist view that sees Christians, and especially those who believe that biblical end-times prophecies are being fulfilled today, as old-fashioned and foolish. Not long ago, I experienced this viewpoint discrimination

16. Eva Cahen, "European Christians Unhappy With Omission in EU Constitution," CNSNews, November 30, 2004, http://www.cnsnews.com// ViewCulture.asp?Page= \\Culture\\archive\\200411\\CUL20041130b.html.

firsthand, when I participated in a documentary entitled, "The Apocalypse Code." This program was supposedly going to examine various end-times views. The resulting documentary, however, was an attack on Bible conservatives by British actor Tony Robbins. After the program aired, I began receiving nasty e-mails from people all over the United Kingdom who had seen the program and who hated the fact that Bible believers even exist!

Prophecy Fulfilled

What they don't know is that their attitude toward Christians and their mocking view of the religious right in America are also fulfillments of prophecy. In Daniel 12:9–10, God told Daniel that, in the time of the end, those who are wise would understand the prophecies Daniel had been shown through the interpretation of his dreams, but the wicked would not understand. That's exactly what we see happening today. To the believer, the world around us makes perfect sense in light of prophecy. Prophecies that at one time would have been confusing, or seemed impossible now make perfect sense in a world where technological advances have changed the nature of war, commerce, politics, and every area of daily life. Yet the wicked go on being wicked and don't understand the signs of the times. They see evil as good and good as evil, and arrogantly believe that they can build their own utopia without the God who created them.

An Associated Press AOL News poll published in January 2007, found that one in four Americans believe that Jesus will return in their lifetimes.[17] However, a Barna research poll taken in 2010 found that only 7 to 10 percent of Americans can give a biblical definition of what it means to be "born again"! This means that somewhere near 30–35 million Americans will suddenly vanish during the Rapture. Imagine for a moment that everyone in your church, or your entire family, suddenly disappeared. Then consider the void that each of them would leave behind. Just among the

---

17. Darlene Superville, "Poll: Americans See Gloom, Doom in 2007," Associated Press, December 31, 2006, http://www.kurtschmidt.com/APDoom_Gloom2007.pdf.

members of your church there might be doctors, policemen, firemen, financial consultants, postal workers, teachers, truck drivers, government employees, politicians, farmers, airline pilots, members of the military, lawyers, and the list goes on. Each of them provides a valuable service to their community, and to their country's ability to function as a civilized nation. The consequences of having such a chunk of America's population suddenly disappear will be disastrous. Crime will likely skyrocket, buildings will burn to the ground, emergency services will cease in many areas, hospitals will be understaffed, our military will be decimated, and the bottom will fall out of the American economy. We will become a Third World country overnight, without a single shot being fired.

America's enemies won't be affected to near the degree that the West, and especially America, will. Muslim countries, which have systematically murdered and pushed out their Christian communities for centuries, will not be immediately impacted. Predominantly Hindu India will be able to recover. Communist China, where atheism and Buddhism flourish, will see little effect from the loss of their Christian population. While Christianity is spreading rapidly in the Communist country, China's enormous population and booming economy could easily absorb the loss of an estimated 100 million Christians that currently make up an underground network of believers in the country. America, however, will be unrecognizable as a country and unable to protect itself. In a situation where America is vulnerable before her enemies and powerless to meet many of the needs of her citizens, she will return to her roots, and look to Europe for protection and help. While Europe will also be affected by the Rapture and the blow it will surely deal to the global economy, their population will not be decimated, and their collateral damage will be far more manageable than that of America.

The Birth of a New World Order

The death of America will set in motion the birth of a new world order, a concept that world leaders have supported since Mikhail

Gorbachev coined the phrase. Events that will immediately follow the Rapture will also contribute to this shift in the balance of power, and the move toward global, dictatorial rule by one man. Revelation 6:7–8 describes the opening of the fourth seal, and the ensuing judgment that will be poured out on an already devastated planet following the Rapture. With the opening of the seal, a quarter of the remaining world population will be killed by the sword, famine, plague, and the wild beasts of the earth. The third trumpet will open to a giant meteor called Wormwood that will be on a collision course with earth (Revelation 8:10). It will find its mark, crashing into the earth with a force greater than that of a nuclear bomb, and many more will die. All total, over half of the population that remains after the Rapture will perish as God judges the wicked, and metes out justice on the world. No wonder so many today prefer to simply ignore the teachings of the ancient prophets and especially those of the Revelation.

With every nation on earth suffering through lawlessness, famine, disease, and warring enemies who will see the Rapture as their opportunity to attack, it won't be a single country that will unite the world under its leadership, but a single man who will display signs and wonders during hopeless times, and promise peace and an end to suffering. That man will arise out of the European Union and take his place at the helm of a unified system of government that is already being formed and prepared for his arrival.

Europe is changing rapidly, and has been for some time. It's as if E.U. leaders have read the Bible, and are preparing for their eventual return to the glory days of the old Roman Empire. One example of such efforts to regain the power and influence they once held can be seen in the creation of the European Rapid Reaction Force (ERRF). In December of 1999, an E.U. declaration began the process of creating a transnational military force that would be managed by the European Union itself, making the E.U. less dependent on NATO, and eventually giving Europe more influence in international affairs.[18] This regional military force was formally founded with an agreement between E.U. countries on its structure and purpose in November 2004. Initially, the ERRF was similar in function to the U.N. peacekeeping forces currently deployed in conflict areas around the globe. Its mandate was strictly humanitarian in nature, and the scope of its mission was limited to peacekeeping operations, rather than combat missions. However, over time, the purpose of the force has evolved to include joint disarmament operations, military advice and assistance tasks, use in fighting the war on terror, and post-conflict stabilization. It is increasingly becoming more of an E.U. military force comparable to the U.S. military than a peacekeeping force used to fill the gaps in NATO's ability to defend and stabilize the region.[19]

As of January 1, 2007, 60,000 soldiers are trained and deployable for missions that can last up to one year. Each unit is composed of some 1,500 troops in reinforced battalions, also known as "packets of force." The primary contributing countries to the buildup of troops are Britain, France, Germany, Italy, Spain, and, eventually, Poland. The remaining smaller countries may in the future form multinational units, such as a Nordic Unit made up of Danish, Swedish, and Finnish troops.[20]

Europe's goal is to maintain a total of 60,000–80,000 troops with a considerable support system behind each unit, as well as air and naval forces as the need arises. ERRF units have already seen successes in Macedonia, where tensions have abated since ERRF troops were sent in, and in Iraq, where they have had success in bringing rest to their assigned areas of operation.[21]

18. Chris Lindborg, "The EU Rapid Reaction Force: Europe Takes on a New Security Challenge," Basic Publications, August 2001, http://www.basicint.org/pubs/Papers/BP37.htm.

19. Ibid.

20. "European Rapid Reaction Force," *Indopedia*, December 04, 2004, http://www.indopedia.org/European_Rapid _ Reaction_Force.html.

21. European Rapid Reaction Force, Wikipedia, March 17, 2007, http://en.wikipedia.org/wiki/European_Rapid_Reaction_Force.

Most feel that the ERRF has weakened NATO by making the E.U. less reliant on the United States. The E.U.'s growing military capabilities have led the United States to propose withdrawing tens of thousands of U.S. troops from bases in Germany, Britain, and Italy.[22] This will greatly reduce U.S. control in any overseas conflict. The perception in Europe is that NATO has made them far too dependent on the national interests of the United States. European Union leadership sees an E.U. military as a monumental step toward wresting power and control from the United States, thereby gaining greater influence in international affairs and regional conflicts on their side of the pond. Should America suffer a devastating attack or economic collapse in the future, Old Europe will possess the military might to fill America's shoes as the world's superpower and police force, and provide the Antichrist with the power and influence the Bible tells us he will assume as he takes the helm of the revived Roman Empire.

As of now, each member state has some control over the use of their troops in ERRF missions. However, the creation of a powerful E.U. presidency may soon change that.

The purpose of the E.U.'s creation was and is, ultimately, to create a European super-state, or "United States of Europe" that can overtake the United States in military might and global decision-making. Part of that shift began in 1999 when Javier Solana became the High Representative for the E.U.'s foreign and security policy, with emergency powers over the military wing of the E.U. given to him through the enactment of Recommendation 666.[23] All that currently remains to create a fully revived Roman Empire is to take Solana's power one step further with the creation of a permanent executive branch of government with far-reaching powers to enforce an E.U. constitution.

---

22. European Rapid Reaction Force, Indopedia.
23. Recommendation 666, on the consequences of including certain functions of WEU in the European Union — reply to the annual report of the Council, Assembly of WEU, http://www.assemblyweu.org/en/documents/sessions_ordinaires/txt/2000/jun00 _txts_adopted.php#P51_.

As Europeans continue down this road toward unification and consolidation of power, they see the value in having an executive branch headed by a single powerful leader capable of speaking for a united Europe. The U.S. president's ability to speak for the nation and negotiate as the head of a representative government gives the United States a diplomatic advantage, and the ability to speak with one voice. Europe recognizes that a similar permanent executive branch, headed by an elected E.U. president, would give them greater influence than they can have with many individual nations speaking for their own interests.

Currently, power is centralized in the form of a rotating E.U. presidency where the leader of each country serves as the E.U. president for a period of six months. This system of sharing power is not only expensive, costing each country tens of millions of euros each time the switch is made, but greatly limits the sitting president's ability to affect foreign policy or influence the decisions of other countries in the short time they are in office.[24] An E.U. president that is elected by the member states for a longer term in office could speak for a unified Europe, act as Commander and Chief over the new E.U. military machine, and become a global force to be reckoned with.

Support for such a move is growing, and E.U. countries, that once opposed the idea as a power grab by the traditional powers of "Old Europe," are predicted to accept the change as part of a slimmed-down version of the E.U. constitution. To ensure its passage, the new E.U. constitution will be renamed a treaty, or charter to avoid any need for the popular referendums that sealed the first E.U. constitutions defeat in 2005.[25]

The British government has already agreed to the changes in how the E.U. will be organized, including a single fixed-term E.U. presidency and a single European "foreign minister" representing a

---

24. Ibid.
25. "EU Presidency: The Big Challenge," *Slovenia Times*, March 08, 2007, http://www.sloveniatimes.com/en/inside.cp2?uid=0785A1D6941AB78DCA8380346 2B D182A&linkid =news&cid =1D973917 D3A1 885B 3840FE67B85C7255.

common E.U. line in international affairs. By June of 2007, E.U. leaders had hoped to hold an intergovernmental conference to thrash out the details, bringing the treaty into force by January 1, 2009.[26]

The E.U. is becoming a diverse but unified power once again, and this poses a serious threat to the power and influence of the United States. As Anthony Gancarski said in his 2003 *CounterPunch* article titled "Blair's War on the Dollar," "The more integration there is between the EU and the UK, the better it is for the Euro and the worse it is for the dollar. Thus it could be said that the E.U. presidency will be strengthened at the expense of the United States and the citizens thereof."

The reunification of Europe and her return to global dominance and power is already happening, just as Daniel prophesied it would during the end times. The Bible is clear that Rome will be the world's superpower in the Last Days, not the United States of America. Perhaps it is a fulfillment of prophecy, then, that America faces threats from so many enemies as the end draws near. I can't predict which of these threats will bring the blow that will end America's dominant position in the world, but we have no reason to believe that one of them won't happen in our future. America is not a major player in the Last Days, or I feel certain the Bible would have included it somewhere in God's prophetic plan for the world. When America does fall from power, whether from a catastrophic attack or as a result of millions of people vanishing during the Rapture, Europe is poised to dominate the world and provide the Antichrist with a position of authority and power from which to rule the world with an iron fist. In the next chapter, we'll take a more detailed look at the global government and global religious system that will be established as the world recovers from the chaos and destruction that will follow the Rapture.

---

26. "Treaty of Lisbon," Wikipedia, February 19, 2008, http://en.wikipedia.org/wiki/Treaty_of_Lisbon.

Chapter 3

THE BIRTH OF THE NEW WORLD ORDER

For as long as I can remember there have been conspiracy theories — theories as to whom or how someone or something is ruling the world behind the scenes. Untold numbers of books and movies abound propagating this theme. Many today believe there is a group of elitists who secretly hand down their plan from one generation of hand-picked propagators to the next and act as puppeteers who are pulling the world's strings. The truth is, there have long been among us those who are proponents of a new world order. They are those elitists who truly believe that they know what's best for the rest of us. They push their agenda not by brute force, but one small step at a time. Through the successes of the European Union, United Nations treaties, the environmental movement, globalization, the interfaith movement, and organizations like the ACLU, they have taken our culture and our society ever closer to the loss of the personal freedoms they once claimed to defend. All of these groups have one thing in common. They want the utopia that so many generations before them have tried in vain to establish. They want world peace, an end to war, an end to poverty, an end to global warming, and an end to every other social or political ill that now plagues this world. That sounds like a great world to live in, but it comes at a very high cost to personal liberties.

They seek to create this new order the only way they can — by legislating, regulating, and negotiating away our right to think or act differently than them. At the same time, they work in concert to bring us ever closer to a global system of government capable of enforcing those infringements on personal liberty and freedom.

The Emerging Global System

In this chapter, we will examine this recent emerging global system. As we've seen, a final world order, or empire, was prophesied long ago by Daniel in his dreams of four world empires that will rule on earth before the reign of Christ in the Millennial Kingdom. Daniel 7:4 speaks of a lion with the wings of an eagle. This lion in Daniel's dream represents the Neo-Babylonian Empire. Daniel's dream in chapter 7 also speaks of a bear, which represents the Medo-Persian Empire that followed the Babylonian Empire, and a leopard, representing the Greek Empire under the rule of Alexander the Great, and eventually the breakup of that empire into four divisions under four of Alexander's generals, as represented by the four heads in Daniel's dream. Verses 7 and 8 go on to describe the fourth empire as a terrifying beast with irresistible power. This beast will have large iron teeth, crushing and devouring its victims and trampling underfoot whatever is left. It will rule the earth in the form of a satanic, final world empire. From the center of this beast, or kingdom, will rise a little horn, that will come up among the other ten horns that represent ten kings. These ten kings will rise to power at the same time. As was discussed earlier, the small horn with "eyes like a man and speaking boastfully" is the Antichrist, who will rise to power from the revived Roman Empire and subdue three of the ten kings. We know this final empire must be a revived form of the Roman Empire, because the old Roman Empire was never defeated. Instead, it imploded from within, which is not the prophesied fate of Daniel's fourth world empire. Therefore, its destruction must come later, and it must rule over the world one final time in the end times, just as Daniel's dream prophesied.

All of us have probably heard sermons, read books, or heard from our religious leaders, friends, or family about this final government that will rule the world in the end times. We've learned that it will herald a global religious system that will be used to control the population of the earth during the Tribulation. It's been my experience that many people simply accept this bit of prophecy interpretation as fact without truly knowing what scriptural support the Bible provides for it. It's unfortunate that prophecy is often neglected as a topic of study in our churches, leaving believers unable to explain the reason for their beliefs to others. Prophecy fulfillment, especially in our time, could be one of the most effective witnessing tools available to us, if pastors and teachers weren't so afraid to teach it, for fear of being labeled a conspiracy theorist or a member of the nutty religious right by our secular society. Unlike other religions, we have as proof the most historically, geographically, and factually accurate book on earth. We need not be afraid to examine the Scriptures and boldly warn others of what is to come. As I explain the verses from Scripture that tell us of the Antichrist's global government, we will see that it is presented to us through the prophets in a logical, amazingly accurate and understandable way. God is not the author of confusion and the Word of God is meant to be used and understood by every one of us, whether we are prophecy scholars, or laypeople.

We've learned through Daniel's dreams that there will be a fourth world empire that will rise up in the end times in the form of the revived Roman Empire. But where exactly does God tell us that this empire, under the leadership of the Antichrist, will rule the entire world and institute a global system of government? This information can be found in several books of the Bible, most notably the Books of Daniel, Revelation, and 2 Thessalonians, among others. What I hope to do here is bring together for you in one place all of the verses that tell us the end-times government of the Tribulation will be a truly global system.

First let's look at Revelation 13:2–4, which reads in part, "The Dragon [Satan] gave the beast [Antichrist] his power and his throne and great authority. One of the heads of the beast seemed to have had a fatal wound, but the fatal wound had been healed. The whole world was astonished and followed the beast." The last sentence of this passage tells us that the Antichrist will not just be followed by those in the E.U., but that the entire world will be astonished by his powers and give their allegiance to him. This verse also tells us that, at some point, the Antichrist will be fatally wounded and then miraculously healed, perhaps mimicking Christ's death and Resurrection on the Cross. Some have also interpreted these verses to mean that the rebirth of the Roman Empire will astonish the world; however, it is clear from other Scripture that the beast is not the Roman Empire, but a man empowered by Satan to rule over the nations in the end times. The Antichrist himself is the object of the world's worship, and it is his signs and wonders that will lead the world to follow him, not a country or government body.

The key point to our studies here, however, is that the whole world will be united in following the beast because of the powers that will be given to him by Satan, and the miracles he will perform for the whole world to see. This is confirmed by 2 Thessalonians 2:9 which states, "The coming of the lawless one will be in accordance with the work of Satan displayed in all kinds of counterfeit miracles, signs and wonders." The fact that the whole world will follow the Antichrist does not, however, tell us that they will follow him under the control and rule of a global system of government. For that, we must read Revelation 13:5–7.

> The beast was given a mouth to utter proud words and blasphemies and to exercise his authority for forty-two months. He opened his mouth to blaspheme God, and to slander his name and his dwelling place and those who live

in heaven. He was given power to make war against the saints and to conquer them. And he was given authority over every tribe, people, language and nation.

These verses clearly tell us that the Antichrist's rule will be over every nation on earth, and he will have authority over every person, regardless of what country they live in, or what sovereignty that country might have enjoyed in the past. In Daniel 7:23 we're also told how the Antichrist will go about usurping power from every nation, government, and leader on the planet. He will rise to power and will "devour the whole earth, trampling it down and crushing it." While this might sound like the Antichrist will launch some kind of massive attack on the entire planet, Daniel 11:21 also says he will not accomplish this through brute force, but by a careful and calculated use of diplomacy. Empowered by Satan, the master deceiver and liar extraordinaire, nations won't just submit reluctantly, they will actually GIVE their power over to the beast.

> The ten horns you saw are ten kings who have not yet received a kingdom, but who for one hour will receive authority as kings along with the beast. They have one purpose and will give their power and authority to the beast (Revelation 17:12–13).

Revelation 13:8–17 says that the False Prophet will be at the Antichrist's side, and working under the Antichrist's authority, he will be responsible for administering a system of marking those who are loyal to the Antichrist.

> All inhabitants of the earth will worship the beast – all whose names have not been written in the book of life belonging to the Lamb that was slain from the creation of the world. He who has an ear let him hear. If anyone is to go into captivity, into captivity he will go. If anyone is to be killed with the sword, with the sword he will be killed. This calls for patient endurance and faithfulness on the part

of the saints. Then I saw another beast, coming out of the earth. He had two horns like a lamb, but he spoke like a dragon. He exercised all the authority of the first beast on his behalf, and made the earth and its inhabitants worship the first beast, whose fatal wound had been healed. And he performed great and miraculous signs, even causing fire to come down from heaven to earth in full view of men. Because of the signs he was given power to do on behalf of the first beast, he deceived the inhabitants of the earth (Revelation 13:8–14).

Global Laws

The False Prophet will be given the authority to create and enforce the global laws requiring every person on the planet to worship the beast and take his mark. Imagine watching on TV as a man who looks as ordinary as any one of us calls down fire from heaven and obliterates anything standing in his master's way of world domination. This miracle-working display will be unlike anything our modern world has ever seen. The saints during the Tribulation period will surely recognize this display of power for what it is, but most of us probably have friends, family, and acquaintances that would undoubtedly conclude from such an astonishing display of power and control over nature that the man capable of this must be some kind of deity. Millions will rally around this dastardly, end-times duo, because in the absence of a strong faith and knowledge of the true God, he will seem to be everything he says he is and then some. Those who are terrified, rather than impressed by the destruction and coercion they see playing out before them, will at least see the threat to their own personal well-being as incentive to obey, and will take the mark to avoid being incinerated where they stand.

The enforcement of laws requiring the worship of the Antichrist on a global scale, and the ability to control who may buy and sell around the world could only be accomplished by a powerful leader at the helm of a global system of government, and through tight control of the world's economy. That the Antichrist will wield this level of power and control is confirmed later in chapter 13 of Revelation. Verses 16 and 17 say, "He also forced everyone small and great, rich and poor, free and slave, to receive a mark on his right hand or on his forehead, so that no one could buy or sell unless he had the mark, which is the name of the beast or the number of his name." We'll look in more detail at this verse in chapter 7, but suffice it to say that there could not be this kind of control over the ability of every person on earth to buy and sell without a global system of tracking and regulating of commerce.

Prophecy from Past to Present

Now that we've examined the scriptural support for a future global government led by the Antichrist and False Prophet, we can look at current events and see just how far the world has come toward the fulfillment of these verses. The creation of the European Union and its cooperation with the rest of the world, and the United Nations, the World Bank, the International Criminal Court, and other global governing bodies are bringing us ever closer to a global system with the revived Roman Empire leading the way as the new dominant world power.

This process of globalization actually began in the middle of the 20th century, when Israel and Rome began to flourish again, and the Holy Lands were established once again as a national homeland for the Jews in 1948. At about the same time, the Roman Empire was being reborn. The Scripture that predicts a revived form of the Roman Empire in the end times began being fulfilled when, in 1950, the European Coal and Steel Community was proposed as a means of unifying Europe during the aftermath of a devastating world war. Forced to strengthen trade in Europe following the war, the creation of the Steel and Coal Community eventually led to the signing of the Treaties of Rome in 1957, which established the European Economic Community, or EEC, and the European Atomic Energy Council (EAEC). The Treaties of Rome, made up of several treaties that were revised and amended over the decades, were the beginning of the reunification of Europe. Subsequent treaties and amendments to those original Treaties of Rome have brought us to where we are today with a united Europe, in the form of the European Union.

The European Union

What was begun in 1957 grew and flourished over time, and in 1973 Denmark, Ireland, and the United Kingdom were added to the European Community, followed by Greece in 1981 and Portugal and Spain in 1986. With these additions to the growing EEC, the original ten nations that still remain are the only states with permanent member status, and Daniel's dreams of a ten-toed statue and a beast with ten horns were starting to be fulfilled. Today, these ten original permanent members make up the military wing of the E.U., and are the only members with veto powers, while the remaining countries hold only observer status as associate members of the Union. The number of nations making up the European Union today has grown to 27, with several other countries likely to join in the near future. These nations now form a union of states spanning the same geographical area once controlled by Alexander the Great during the glory days of the Old Roman Empire.

In addition to geographical unification, the 90s began the process of forming the regional economy and system of government that has become the template for the regionalization of the rest of the planet, and the eventual global government of prophecy. The most notable economic unification of Europe occurred in 1993, with the signing of the Maastricht Treaty, which made the treaty of Rome obsolete by establishing a basis for a common currency, a common judiciary, a common foreign policy, and even an official common military defense wing of the E.U. This transformed the European Community into the European Union, and a truly regional government with growing influence and power in the world was born.

By unifying all the nations in Europe politically and economically, Europe successfully prevented another bloody world war. However, the original and current purpose behind the E.U.'s creation has always been to bring from the ashes of World War II the rise of a new European super-state, or "United States of Europe," as it's been called. In more recent history, the ambitions of E.U. leaders have been driven by a desire to regain the power and prestige they once had before the United States rose to power and won the Cold War. European countries have remained in the background, and watched jealously as the United States rose to become a super power in what is considered to be a short period of time, historically. They view the tremendous U.S. influence on the world stage as a power too frequently abused, and an influence that more appropriately rests in the hands of the secular, progressive elites of the European Union.

One such elite leader, Javier Solana, became the High Representative for the E.U.'s Foreign and Security Policy, receiving his power in 2000 through the E.U. legislation ironically titled "Recommendation 666." This recommendation gave Solana emergency powers over the military wing of the European Union. It was the first real step toward creating an executive branch of the European Union, whose powers have grown over the years and gained in influence internationally. All that remains to create a true executive branch of government, that will rival the United States in power, is the creation of a permanent E.U. presidency a position that could become an ideal office for introducing the Antichrist to the world, and thrust him into power at a time of chaos and global war.

The year 2007 marked the 50th anniversary of the Treaties of Rome. Now, 50 years after the first treaty was signed, the European Union encompasses more than 540 million people and has a gross domestic product larger than that of the United States. As the borders have been expanding, there have also been political battles being waged over a European constitutional treaty that will officially unify the European Union under one set of laws, and will be constitutionally binding on all nations in the Union.

The first attempt at passing a European constitution was made in 2005, but because it was presented to the member states as a constitution rather than a reform treaty, it required ratification by a consensus vote in each member country. The French and Dutch voted to reject the constitution in 2005, effectively defeating it, and catapulting the European Union into crisis mode. While the objectors succeeded in delaying the goals of the constitution, its future ratification is inevitable. Undeterred, E.U. politicians found a way around the ratification process that originally put the constitution up for a vote by every person in the Union. By constructing what amounts to a new constitution in the form of the "Lisbon Treaty," they retained the content of the constitution, while only requiring approval by each nation's parliament. Instead of requiring a national referendum, each state will decide independently how they will present the treaty to their citizens, and what method of ratification is most appropriate for their citizens. Leaders in Britain have already stated that they don't believe the treaty meets the bar of fundamental constitutional reform, and therefore should not require a referendum. The treaty will instead be debated by the British parliament, and will require only a majority parliamentary approval for passage.[1] By giving each nation the power to determine what route they will take toward the Lisbon Treaty's passage, the European Commission put negotiating power back in the hands of the elites, rather than in the hands of the people.

Once this new "Reform Treaty," as it's commonly called, passes, it will define the powers of the European Union, determine where and when the E.U. can act, as well as dictate when permanent members will retain their right to veto E.U. policies and legislation.[2]

1. "New Treaty Same as E.U. Constitution," Reuters UK, January 20, 2008, http://uk.reuters.com/ArticlePrint?articleId=UKL2046 388420080120.

2. "What the E.U. Constitution Says," BBC News, June 22, 2004, http://bbc.co.uk/mpapps/pagetools/print/news.bbc.co.uk.

In its final form, the treaty will likely give the E.U. extended rights into justice policy, especially immigration law, and will expand on the existing E.U. powers to legislate over external trade and customs policy, the internal market, monetary policy, agriculture, and many areas of domestic law, including labor laws. This puts wide-ranging powers in the hands of a regional government for the first time in centuries. Just as Alexander the Great and his generals ruled over the entire civilized world of that day, E.U. leaders will exercise control over a revived form of the same empire.

As I stated previously, another function of the constitutional treaty will be to establish a permanent E.U. presidency to replace the existing rotating presidency that currently passes from each permanent member nation on a schedule. This will bring continuity to E.U. leadership, and a two and one-half year term, which is renewable once, will give the E.U. president far greater influence and symbolism in international affairs. It is highly likely that the final form of this office will provide a position of leadership to the future Antichrist, albeit on a far greater scale during the chaos of the Islamic invasion of Israel and time of Tribulation on earth that will follow.

A position ideally suited for the False Prophet will also be introduced in the new treaty in the form of a foreign minister's office. The E.U. president, with the agreement of the E.U. Council, will appoint a Union Minister of Foreign Affairs who will conduct the Union's common foreign and security policy. The powers of the external affairs member of the European Commission and the High Representative on Foreign Policy will be combined to create a far more prominent role, much like the U.S. office of vice president, except with perhaps greater powers and more responsibility. Under the treaty, the new foreign minister will have a great deal of political clout, money, and even his own diplomatic service. He will speak for the E.U. at the United Nations, and facilitate defense cooperation among the E.U. member nations. The creation of such a position is a step toward creating a political office capable of implementing a system of marking loyal citizens and policing the world.

The E.U. Constitution may have failed when France and the Netherlands rejected it in 2005, but it still lives on, almost completely unchanged, in the form of the Lisbon Treaty. On October 19, 2007, the Lisbon Treaty was agreed upon by the leaders of all 27 E.U. member states. It was agreed that the treaty will replace the E.U. constitution that was roundly rejected in 2005, so long as each nation can at least reach unanimity in a parliamentary vote. Since the leaders of all 27 member nations have already approved the final wording of the treaty, and are eager to see its passage, we can assume those leaders will make its passage all but guaranteed by using a method of ratification most likely to win unanimous support. When the treaty comes up for a vote the next time around, governments will be desperate to avoid the same disastrous results and embarrassment that followed the previous attempt to unite E.U. nations around a regional constitution. Fully aware that the world will judge the E.U.'s power and influence based on the member nations' ability to rally around a set of common guiding principles and laws, leaders like the former British Prime Minister Gordon Brown are insisting that the treaty be ratified by parliament rather than a popular vote of the people.[3]

In addition to creating a common set of laws for the union, the euro was launched to rival the U.S. dollar, and is, in fact, overtaking the dollar as the currency of choice in global markets. Meanwhile, the greenback's value continues to plummet under the strain of unmanaged national debt and decades of being propped up by the dollar's exclusive use in oil sales.

Financial supremacy and political unification are not, however, Europe's only goals. For some time, E.U. leaders have been eager to challenge America's dominance in defense and security. Like the defeated E.U. constitution, the Lisbon Treaty will completely alter the structure of E.U. institutions and how they currently operate, especially in the areas of defense. The Maastricht Treaty of 1992 was the first to contain provisions on the E.U.'s responsibility for all questions

---

3. "Taking Europe into the 21st Century," *Europa*, http://europa.eu/lisbon_treaty/take/index_en.htm.

relating to E.U. security, including a common defense policy. Then in 1997, the Treaty of Amsterdam incorporated Western Europe's mainly peacekeeping and crisis management "Petersberg tasks" into the Treaty on the European Union. This was followed in 1998 by an Anglo-French agreement that declared a need for the "capacity for autonomous action, backed up by credible military forces." This unifying defense strategy was agreed upon at the Cologne Summit in 1999, and effectively achieved by the Marseilles Declaration of 2000. Finally, in the 2000 Treaty of Nice, E.U. member states formally decided to create a rapid reaction force (RRF) of 60,000 men brought together from the military assets of each of the member states.

One of the agencies established in 2004 under the E.U.'s new Foreign and Security Policy was the European Defense Agency, based in Brussels. Reporting to the Council of the European Union, the EDA serves all European Union member states except Denmark, who opted out. Its four functions are to develop defense capabilities, promote defense research and technology, promote armaments cooperation, and create a competitive European defense equipment market, while strengthening the European defense, technological, and industrial base. We have seen these goals being fulfilled in the purchase of far greater numbers of U.S. aircraft and equipment that are being used to bring the E.U. military into this century, and deploy E.U. troops to conflict areas around the world.[4]

The E.U.'s defense policy currently aims to focus on the four priority areas of police protection, rule of law, civilian administration, and civil protection capabilities, as well as to further the principles of the charter of the United Nations, while complementing NATO in the region. While member states are allowed command over the forces they voluntarily provide to the E.U.'s military units, the E.U. treaty also dictates that each member state "shall support the Union's common foreign and security policy actively and unreservedly in a spirit of loyalty and mutual solidarity." This makes the E.U. military

---

4. "European Defense Agency," Wikepedia, http://en.wikipedia. org/wiki/
   European_Defense_Agency.

force a unified military wing, under the control of Union leaders, which they hope will eventually rival the U.S. military in readiness, and bring them far greater international influence.

The E.U. currently spends 160 billion euros on defense, and it is taking greater responsibility and a more active role in international military affairs, which continues to give them greater political weight in the international debate over when and how to use force, combat terrorism, and deal with regional conflicts. As you can see, the E.U.'s defense policy is one of both regional and global impact, just as we would expect to see in Europe as we come closer to the end times.

In a strategy paper written by then E.U. High Representative Javier Solana, the European Union presented its international goals as being to develop a stronger international society, well-functioning international institutions, and a rule-based international order. The document goes on to explain that the E.U. is committed to upholding and developing International Law — a goal that is being promoted through support for the International Criminal Court. They also hold the United Nations Charter to be the fundamental framework for international relations. The U.N. charter is a document that is hostile to Christians, attacks religious freedoms, and sets as its objective the creation of a united utopian planet living under one set of international rules, as laid out by the unelected elites at the United Nations. Solana maintains in his policy paper that the U.N. Security Council has the primary responsibility for the maintenance of international peace and security, and promises E.U. support and assistance in equipping the U.N. to fulfill its responsibilities and to act effectively. The E.U. wants strong international organizations that can be effective in confronting threats and making international regimes comply with international law by acting forcefully when U.N. rules are broken.[5] Their regional ambitions are also global ambitions, and the U.N. is the perfect global body to eagerly

5. "An International Order Based on Effective Multilateralism, A secure Europe in a Better World," European Security Strategy — Brussels, 12/12/2003, drafted under E.U. High Representative Javier Solana, http://www.acronym.org.uk/docs/0312/doc11.htm.

support, if Europe wants to establish a new international order and merge regional constitutions into international law.

These international goals and the E.U.'s support for a stronger, more authoritative United Nations are indicative of their desire to extend their power and influence on a global scale. Europe longs for a return to their status as a world empire, and they recognize that the best way to compete with the United States' power and influence in international affairs is to strengthen global agencies and organizations, as well as to build up their own military wing that will rival the U.S. military machine in conflict resolution and peacekeeping. Toward this end, on June 3, 1999, the Cologne European Council launched a project of developing an independent European Security and Defense Policy (ESDP). The goal of this policy was and is to strengthen the E.U.'s external ability to act through the development of civilian and military capabilities for international conflict prevention and crisis management.[6]

The New Foreign Minister position, first introduced in the 2004 E.U. constitution, would enjoy wide-ranging powers over defense policy, as well as the operations of a unified E.U. military force. As many as 1,500 battle groups are already prepared for rapid deployment to trouble spots in the world, and their military capabilities have already been successfully tested in the takeover of the NATO peacekeeping mission in Bosnia Herzegovina in 2005. E.U. rapid reaction forces have also seen great success in Iraq, where they quickly stabilized large areas of the country during the chaos that followed the U.S. invasion. Using a "single set of forces" principle, the E.U. hopes to utilize NATO equipment and intelligence when needed, while maintaining a right and an ability to act on its own in defense of the E.U., and in response to regional conflicts that affect the Union. In other words, the United States will strengthen their capabilities, while giving up many of the decision-making powers they've historically held.

---

6. "E.U. Security and Defense Policy," January 6, 2005, http://www.euractive. com/en/security/eusecuritydefensepolicy/article.

Efforts to Create a Global Government

The ability to enforce the worship of the Antichrist on a global scale, and to regulate who may buy or sell around the world could only be accomplished in a global system of government, and through tight control of the world's economy. We see efforts underway now to create this global government and economic system through the creation of an E.U. super-state and the efforts of the United Nations, in concert with the World Bank and International Criminal Court, and it's all happening just as the E.U. is becoming a union of nations under the leadership of ten permanent members and one head in the form of an E.U. presidency. The final world government will be a diverse group of nations — a mixture of iron and clay just like in Nebuchadnezzar's dream — under the leadership of the Antichrist and His False Prophet.

The positions of leadership, government agencies, and unified military forces and currency are already being created on a regional basis in the European Union. This same regionalization process and globalization of the world's economy is happening now. In chapter 8 we will look more closely at the economic integration happening around the world, and how this form of globalization and international cooperation is already establishing a system of commerce, and the technological tools that will be needed to enforce strict restrictions on who is able to buy and sell around the world. In all of these areas, Europe is paving the way toward a technology-driven world that gives regional governments greater control over every person on the planet.

Chapter 4

THE ISLAMIC INVASION
OF ISRAEL

The summer of 2006 was a preview of coming events. My family had just returned from Israel in late June. While in the land, I had conversed with several of my Israeli contacts about the increased rhetoric and threats coming from Lebanon, Syria, and Hamas controlling Gaza. The talk was that Israel's enemies were planning to kidnap Israeli soldiers and use them as bargaining chips for additional concessions from Israel. This threat had led to increased caution among the Israeli military. However, before we had departed for home we heard the report of the capture of a young Israeli soldier, Gilad Shalit. The following days brought news of additional kidnappings and heightened tension in the Middle East. Then on July 12, Lebanon began firing rockets into northern Israel. In the following days, as Israel began to respond, I began to hear and read of preachers saying this is Armageddon. The next month would prove to be a trying time in Israel as their enemies rallied with continuous calls for the destruction of the Jews. The question is, was it Armageddon? The answer is no! That said, for the first time the world witnessed the geopolitical alignment of nations prophesied by the ancient prophet Ezekiel 25 centuries ago. The Bible clearly reveals God's plan for the future of Israel and this earth.

After the Rapture of the Church, not a single born-again Christian will be left behind. That's not to say there won't be a large number of people around the world who, upon learning that their family and friends have vanished, won't suddenly realize their mistake and give their life to Christ. There will surely be those who make that decision, albeit too late. Unfortunately, while their salvation will be secure, they will be doomed to suffer through seven years of Tribulation like the world has never seen. It will be seven difficult years before they will be rejoined with their loved ones at the glorious appearing and the final battle of Armageddon.

The world is finally going to get exactly what it wants — a secular world without Christians. The utopia they've longed for, where tolerance and political correctness reign will seem to be within their grasp. However, following the Rapture, the world will be thrown into utter chaos. Imagine a world where a large percentage of the population simply vanishes. Bus drivers, airplane pilots, teachers, bankers, and civil servants will simply vanish from their cars, airplanes, classrooms, and jobs. The world as we know it will come to a screeching halt.

Do you remember the jubilation in the streets of Muslim countries when the Twin Towers in New York came crashing down on September 11, 2001? Imagine the celebration in the streets of Baghdad, Iran, and even Europe when the U.S. economy collapses. Muslim extremists around the globe will see it as Allah's judgment upon the West.

Muslim countries, of course, will not see the level of devastation that the Western world will have to endure. Over the centuries, due to persecution and Islamic law, Islamic countries have seen their Christian and Jewish populations dwindle as Jewish citizens returned to Israel and Christians fled for a safer place to raise their families. In the eyes of Islamic terrorists, the world will suddenly change for the better. Countries like Iran will see the chaotic world around them as an opportunity for conquest, and they will seize that opportunity. As we'll see in this chapter, the way is already being paved for a regional war in the Middle East that will usher in the reign of the Antichrist and a global government that will seem to be the world's only hope of returning to some sense of normalcy. The stage is set for the Rapture to happen at any moment, and the Middle East is a powder keg waiting to go off.

The Rapture is going to set in motion a series of events that will usher in the seven-year Tribulation. As believers, we may or may not be here to experience these events. It's my personal belief that we won't be here to experience the horrors that will follow the rise of Antichrist, nor will we witness the war that will break out in the Middle East during the chaotic aftermath of the Rapture. We are, however, witnessing the beginning of that war. It's being played out on our TV screens 24 hours a day in news coverage of the war on terror.

God has revealed a great deal of His future plan to us through the Bible, and part of that plan includes a major escalation of the already raging battles in the Middle East. The wars in Iraq and Afghanistan, and the war on terror, are just the beginning. We can know this because Ezekiel 38 and 39 tell us that there will be a regional war in the Middle East following the Rapture. This war will remove any doubt from people's minds that we are in fact in the middle of World War III. Even Ayman Al Zawahiri, Al Qaeda's current leader, has referred to the war on terror as World War III. A third world war has certainly begun. The West is just late showing up. We have not realized yet that we are at war with a violent ideology. If western nations continue to wage a politically correct campaign against the satanic religion of Islam, we are all going to pay a price for our lack of due diligence and inability to face reality. A regional war in the Middle East is inevitable, but how much we suffer as a nation in the meantime is within our power to control, as long as we're willing to wake up and face the real enemy head-on.

Controversy in the Islamic World

Before we examine Ezekiel's prophecies, I want to make it very clear that I do not hate Muslims. I have hundreds of Muslim friends in the Middle East, and they are good and decent people. There are those in the Muslim world who don't subscribe to the terrorist's ideology of death, conquest, and conversion by the sword. I'm not speaking about individual Muslims, when I speak out against the religion of Islam. Many Muslims in America have come here longing for a better life, but there is a second group of people who have infiltrated our borders for the purpose of destroying our way of life. While we've abandoned our immigration laws and put at risk our own security, they have taken advantage of our naiveté, crossed our borders, and now seek to destroy us from within. They are the enemy among us. Once again, there is a clear differentiation between these two groups.

However, the fact remains that the peaceful Muslims among us are in disagreement with their own scripture, the Quran, and their founding prophet, Muhammad, when they choose to denounce violence against those of other faiths. As we will see, among Islam's most core doctrines is the belief that the religion of Allah will dominate the earth, and Islamic law will be imposed on a global scale by a leader who bears a striking resemblance to the Antichrist, as he is described in the Bible. It is this belief that will draw the Islamic world into a regional war in the Middle East, and fulfill the end-times prophecies given by the Lord to Ezekiel.

Prophecy Concerning the Islamic War

In Ezekiel 38 and 39, the Lord Himself spoke to Ezekiel of a future regional war that would take place in the Middle East, following the Rapture of the Church. Verses one through six give us some of the details about this future war.

> The word of the LORD came to me: "Son of man, set your face against Gog, of the land of Magog, the chief

prince of Meshech and Tubal; prophesy against him and say: 'This is what the Sovereign LORD says: I am against you, O Gog, chief prince of Meshech and Tubal. I will turn you around, put hooks in your jaws and bring you out with your whole army — your horses, your horsemen fully armed, and a great horde with large and small shields, all of them brandishing their swords. Persia, Cush and Put will be with them, all with shields and helmets, also Gomer with all its troops, and Beth Togarmah from the far north with all its troops—the many nations with you (Ezekiel 38:1–6).

Before we look at these verses in detail, it's important not to confuse this regional war with the battle of Armageddon. In Revelation, chapter 16, the battle of Armageddon is described as a global war between good and evil. All of the nations of the world who followed the Antichrist during the Tribulation will come together to fight a final battle against Jesus Christ, who will return in the air with His Church. These verses in Revelation must be describing a different war, fought at a different time, because the war described in Ezekiel will be a regional conflict between Israel and a coalition of surrounding nations, and not a war involving the entire world. The war described in Ezekiel also takes place during the end times before judgment has been poured out on the nations, and well before Christ returns to establish His millennial Kingdom.

There's one more important distinction to be made before we delve into a study of these verses. In chapter 20 of Revelation, another battle is mentioned involving Gog of Magog. This also is not a reference to the war that's being described in Ezekiel 38. Instead, it's describing a final battle when Satan will be loosed a final time at the end of the one thousand year reign of Christ on earth. Once again, these battles take place at different times, and involve different participants.

Now that we understand what this war is not, let's look at what it is. What's being described in chapter 38 is an end-times scenario that God Himself imparted to His servant Ezekiel, 2,500 years ago, and the intended audience is a future generation that will live through the end times. We know with certainty that this prophecy was intended for a future generation, because what is described in these verses has never happened before in history. We're also told in verse eight that this war will take place after many days and in future years. I believe that those "many days" have now passed, and we are the generation that will see this prophecy fulfilled. The time is very near for an escalation in the Middle East conflict that will change the world forever.

As I study Scripture, I like to look for key words and phrases that might add insight into what God is trying to convey to us. It's worth noting that six times in these verses, Ezekiel writes, "This is what the sovereign Lord says." This is a reminder to us that end-time events are not going to originate in the minds of men, but they originated in the mind of God. God has already preordained these things to happen, and participants in this scenario have already been determined. This is so that a future generation can know what to watch for as events begin to unfold. However, you'll notice we're given names like Cush, Put, and Tubal that sound totally foreign to us today. How can we know who in the world these people are? Fortunately, God gave us a table of nations in the form of genealogies that can help us trace these names to their current identities in our day. We've all probably come across these lists of names and ancestors when we've decided to read the Bible from beginning to end. We get to the tenth chapter of Genesis and about 12 verses in we sheepishly flip ahead to the next chapter. Well, it turns out, while admittedly boring to read, all of those names come in very handy as we study Bible prophecy.

In Genesis chapter 10, God gives us the information we need to determine who the nations in Ezekiel 38 are. The names of countries, tribes, and kingdoms change through the centuries, but by starting with the ancient name we can trace their descendants through the pages of history to their current identities and locations.

After the Flood, Noah's sons Shem, Ham, and Japheth began to populate the world. These descendants of Noah spread out into the world to form their own kingdoms and nations. It's among this list of descendants that we find mention of the ten nations that will form a coalition to attack Israel. The first name mentioned is Gog of the land of Magog. Herodotus, the fifth-century historian known as the father of history, recorded that the Magogians were also known as the Scythians. This is confirmed by the Jewish historian Josephus who wrote, "Magog founded the Magogians, called Scythians by the Greeks. Scythians were a nomadic tribe who inhabited the ancient territory from central Asia across the southern part of ancient Russia." Magog today is modern-day Russia, including the former Soviet republics of Kazakhstan, Kyrgyzstan, Uzbekistan, Turkmenistan, Tajikistan, and possibly northern parts of Afghanistan. All of these nations that make up the land of Magog have one thing in common — Islam. Militant Islam has been on the rise in these countries since the fall of the Soviet Union, when Islam no longer had to be practiced secretly. Radical Islamic groups such as the Islamic Renaissance Party, the Islamic Movement of Uzbekistan, and Hizb ut-Tahrir al-Islam have been working to reunite Muslims in central Asia with those living in Russia, as well as to develop closer ties to Iran and Turkey.

Enemies of Israel Unite

There is some debate among scholars as to the translation of the Hebrew word *Gog* in these verses, but I believe that Gog should be a proper noun as the Greek texts translate it. The Greek word for Gog is the proper name Ros, and it provides further evidence that Gog is, in fact, a reference to modern-day Russia. The ancient Sarmatians were known as Ras, Rashu, and Rus, and they inhabited Rasapu, which is now Southern Russia. This also fits perfectly with verses 6 and 15 of Ezekiel 38, which state that the invaders will come from the far north. Today's map puts Russia north of every nation mentioned in the coalition, and north of Israel.

If you add to this evidence the fact that Russia is not an ally of the United States or Israel, it's easy to imagine a leader rising from this part of the world to bring together an Islamic coalition that will invade Israel. Russia consistently sides with Muslim countries at the United Nations, sides with the Palestinians in the Middle East conflict, and joins China in opposing the United States and Britain in the war on terror. Their support, however, is not limited to political backing. Russia is a major supplier of arms and military technology for Arab countries in the region. Islamic countries have no shortage of men willing to sacrifice their lives in an invasion of Israel, but they need Russia to equip them for 21st-century warfare. With Russia's military decimated by the economic collapse that accompanied the fall of communism, they are only too happy to sell their massive inventory of weapons to Israel's arch enemy.

In verses 2 and 6, we are given the names Meshech and Tubal, which are the fifth and sixth sons of Japheth. Ezekiel 27:13 also mentions Meshech and Tubal as being trading partners with Tyre, or modern-day Lebanon. According to Josephus, Japheth settled his people north of the Black Sea in what is today Romania and the Ukraine, while Japheth's sons, Tubal and Meshech settled south of the Black Sea. It's likely that Meshech and Tubal are referring to the ancient Moshi/Mushki and Tubalu/Tibareni who inhabited the area primarily south of the Caspian Sea and the Dead Sea. Today, these nations would occupy part of Turkey, parts of southern Russia, and northern Iran. Once again, these are all areas with a Muslim majority.

Ezekiel 38:6 adds Gomer and Beth-togarmah to the coalition of invading nations. Gomer was the first son of Japheth, and the Gomerites are also known as the ancient Cimmerians. The first historical record of the Cimmerians appears in Assyrian annals, where it is recorded that in the year 714 B.C., the Cimmerians lived in Mannae, which is located in the present-day northwestern province of West Azerbaijan in Iran. The geographer Ptolemy also placed the Cimmerian city of Gomara in this region. Later records show that after a series of successful invasions, the Cimmerians conquered Paphlagonia in modern Turkey. Finally, the Cimmerians can be traced to eastern Europe where even today Jewish immigrants are referred to as Ashkenazi Jews after Gomer's son Ashkenaz.

Beth-togarmah was also located in Turkey during Ezekiel's time. Since three of these tribes of people can be traced to Turkey, we can safely assume that Turkey will be a willing participant in the invasion. Current circumstances in Turkey lend this view further credence. Turkey is linked to central Asia both ethnically and linguistically, and support for Islamic rule in Turkey has grown exponentially as radical groups have pushed politics closer to the anti-Israel rhetoric of their Arab allies. Like many other Muslim countries, Turkey also has strong ties to Russia through defense contracts and weapon sales.

In verse 5, we're introduced to three more names. Persia is an easy one. Many Iranians will quickly correct you, if you refer to them as Arabs. Over 50 percent of the population are actually Persian and speak Farsi instead of the Arabic spoken in other Islamic countries. Iran once made up a large part of the Persian Empire, and only became known as Iran in 1935 when, after World War I, the Allies divided up the Ottoman Empire and Iran's leader Reza Shah renamed it Iran. Following the Iranian Revolution in 1979, Iran was renamed again as the Islamic Republic of Iran.

Iran has been a supporter of terrorism for decades, and openly funds groups like Hezbollah, Hamas, and Al Qaeda in their fight against Israel and the United States. The Iranian President Mahmoud Ahmadinejad has publicly vowed to "wipe Israel off the map," and is currently enriching uranium for a nuclear weapons program that would give him the means to do just that. Ahmadinejad sees the threat of mutual destruction as an incentive for launching a nuclear attack, not a deterrent, and he brags often of the thousands of Iranian men who are lined up ready to become martyrs for Allah. As we saw in the last chapter, Ahmadinejad fancies himself a kind of John the Baptist for the Mahdi, Islam's messiah, who will appear in the last days and return Islam to its glory days of conquest and power.

Joining the coalition with Iran will be Cush and Put. When the Book of Ezekiel was written, Cush was located in modern-day Sudan, yet another Islamic country. Sudan also harbors numerous terrorist groups, including the National Islamic Front, and being a former home to Bin Laden himself, Al Qaeda also has a presence within Sudan's borders. Sudan, like so many other Islamic countries in the region, has strong ties to Iran, and trades military supplies for Iranian docking rights along its Red Sea shipping routes. Sudan's military dictatorship wouldn't hesitate to join Iran in a campaign to dominate the Middle East and destroy the nation of Israel.

Ancient Put was located in the area just west of Egypt, or in what is now Libya. Libya, too, has a long history of connections to terrorism, and joins the Arab world in refusing to acknowledge Israel's right to even exist.

Verses 13 and 14 introduce three nations that will appear to question the invaders' actions. These three nations were called Sheba, Dedan, and Tarshish in Ezekiel's time. Today, Sheba is located in Yemen, and Dedan is now Saudi Arabia. Tarshish is most commonly agreed to be ancient Tartessus, which was in the area of present-day Spain in western Europe. In Ezekiel's time, Tarshish was in the farthest west regions of the known world. By referring to Tarshish and all her merchants, Ezekiel may have been indicating that western Europe will join with Saudi Arabia in denouncing the invasion, while remaining neutral when it comes to actually actively opposing it.

It's in these kinds of details that Bible prophecy becomes such a powerful witnessing tool. The accuracy with which prophecy is being fulfilled is truly amazing. Saudi Arabia is the only Arab nation to consistently side with the West against radical Islamic elements around the world. It's true that Saudi Arabia is far from a true ally of the West. However, they have an interest in not letting radical Islam become too powerful in their own country. The ruling monarchy fears groups like Al Qaeda, who see Saudi Arabia's oil ties to the West as an evil act of betrayal.

As with Saudi Arabia, Yemen allows the U.S. military to use their ports and has a vested interest in at least appearing to side with the West. Both nations, while funding terrorism and supporting the ideology that feeds it, will do as they've always done and speak out against such an attack, while secretly supporting it.

Western Europe can also be counted on to publicly oppose the invasion, while at the same time opposing any action to prevent it. They will side with Islam, in much the same way that they have chosen sides in the wars in Afghanistan and Iraq, by doing nothing more than verbally chastising the nations who have been waging a terrorist war on Israel for decades.

Finally, Ezekiel concludes his list of invading nations with the words, "and many nations with you." The nations that have been given to us with much specificity in Ezekiel are somewhat distant from Israel. When God tells us there will be many nations with them, He may be referring to the other Islamic countries that are in closer proximity to Israel. Other nations that would likely join a coalition of Islamic invaders are Iraq, Syria, Jordan, and Egypt, as well as the Palestinians. All of these countries are governed by the laws of Islam and would be eager to join a coalition of invading countries, just as they did in 1948 and 1967 when the Arab world first attacked Israel with the same goal of eliminating any Jewish presence in the Middle East.

We've actually seen a similar alliance once before. During the Gulf War in the early 1990s, the United States was allied with European countries, with tacit support from countries like Saudi Arabia in the Middle East. Siding with Iraq were Russia, Iran, Sudan, Libya, and other Islamic countries.

The following table summarizes what we've learned from Ezekiel about a coming Russo-Islamic invasion of Israel in the end times.

ANCIENT NAME	MODERN NATION
Rosh	Russia
Magog	Central Asia
Meshech	Turkey
Tubal	Turkey, Southern Russia
Persia	Iran
Ethiopia (Cush)	Sudan
Put	Libya
Gomer	Eastern Europe
Beth-Togarmah	Turkey
Many peoples with you	Other Islamic nations

The stage is being set for these Islamic countries, led by Russia, to attack the nation of Israel. These countries think that it is their idea to invade Israel and finally realize their goal of destroying the Jewish homeland, but Ezekiel 38:4 tells us that God will put hooks in their jaws and bring them out. God is going to use these nations to bring about His end-times plan for the world.

We can look back to the Book of Exodus for an example of God using someone to complete His plan. Pharaoh thought it was his idea to free the Israelites from bondage in Egypt, but in actuality God used Pharaoh to complete His plan for the Jews. In the same way, God will use these nations. How can a loving God use people to create war? God is the Creator, and we're the clay. If God chooses one person in a noble way and another person in a different way, He can do what He wants. He already knows the hearts of individuals and the choices they will make. We should consider that God has a score to settle with these countries. Russia and the Muslim world have tortured and tormented the Jewish people for centuries, and the Book of Joel makes it clear that God will judge those who persecute His people, just as Genesis says that God will bless those who bless Israel, and curse those who curse her. God is going to judge these nations and avenge the Jewish people through a massive defeat on the mountains of Israel.

Israel Can't Be Touched

Six times in these verses God says that He will lead this coalition to war so that "they may know that I am Lord." When Israel is attacked, God will step out of heaven and bring about the complete destruction of the invading forces. It won't be the might of Israel that subdues them, but the very hand of God. In verse 18, we learn how God will bring about their destruction. His hot anger will be aroused, and He will cause a violent earthquake that will make every creature on earth tremble at His presence. Mountains will be overturned, cliffs will crumble, and every wall will fall to the ground. God will execute judgment on them with a plague of bloodshed, torrents of rain, hailstones, fire from heaven, and burning sulfur. On the mountains of Israel, Russia and the nations who joined with her will be utterly defeated in much the same way Sodom and Gomorrah were destroyed.

In chapter 39 we read that the carnage will be so great that it takes seven months just to bury the dead, and the people of Israel will use the invading force's weapons for fuel for a period of seven years. It's interesting to note here that the shelf life of a nuclear implosion device is seven years. Of course, the Tribulation will also last seven years, so this is further evidence that the invasion of Israel will occur just after the Rapture and at the beginning of the Tribulation or in the interim period between the Rapture and the signing of the peace treaty that marks the beginning of the Tribulation. It's possible that undetonated nuclear weapons will become a source of fuel for Israel that will last them through the seven-year Tribulation. Tritium gas, found in nuclear weapons, has many uses and poses less of a radiation risk to humans. Along with tritium gas, Israel will likely be able to use the fuel from Russian tanks and other military equipment. With the destruction wrought by this Middle East war, oil will likely be in high demand.

Nuclear Warfare

We know the attack will be a nuclear attack, because in chapter 39, verse 11, we see that the fallen invading forces will block travel, and it will take seven months to bury the dead and cleanse the land. Verse 14 continues, "Men will be regularly employed to cleanse the land. Some will go throughout the land and, in addition to them, others will bury those that remain on the ground. At the end of the seven months they will begin their search. As they go through the land and one of them sees a human bone, he will set up a marker beside it until the gravediggers have buried it in the Valley of Hamon Gog. And so they will cleanse the land." In the case of a nuclear attack, great care would need to be taken to bury the dead because of the radiation that will be present within the blast zone, and that will contaminate the bodies themselves. It's easy to imagine that a nuclear attack, using Russia's Cold War military stockpiles, would block travel through the contaminated mountains surrounding Israel. After seven months of preparation, and allowing enough time for contamination levels to subside, special hazardous materials task forces from the IDF, and possibly other countries, would be needed to locate and dispose of the contaminated bodies. Only in our time could such a recovery mission truly make sense.

You might be wondering what motives Russia and the Islamic world would have for launching an invasion. God gives us the answer in Ezekiel 38, starting in verse 12. The current situation in the Middle East and the ambitions of Islamic countries around the world fit perfectly into God's prophetic plan for our time.

As we've seen, the common denominator in all of these invading countries is the satanic religion of Islam. Even in Russia, a large segment of the population is Muslim, and the southern former republics of the Soviet Union have a Muslim population of over 60 million. It is their beliefs as Muslims that provide the motive for attacking.

Let's look first at verses 12 through 13, "I will plunder and loot and turn my hand against the resettled ruins and the people gathered from the nations, rich in livestock and goods, living at the center of the land. Sheba and Dedan and the merchants of Tarshish and all her villages will say to you, 'Have you come to plunder? Have you gathered your hordes to loot, to carry off silver and gold, to take away livestock and goods and to seize much plunder?' "

The armies of Islam have a long history of plundering and looting as they conquer foreign lands. The Repentance Surat in the Quran records several battles in Islam's history where the victims were given three choices — accept Islam, pay a tax for your unbelief (the jizya), or die by the sword. After one such battle, Muhammad proclaimed the ordinance, "Know that whatsoever thing ye plunder, verily one fifth thereof is for God and for the prophet."[1] The remaining spoils were to be divided among the warriors.

We can also look to a more recent example of this practice. Before the Arab countries that surround Israel launched a united attack on Israel in 1948 and again in 1967, the Arabs living within Israel were warned to flee, and were promised Israeli homes and land upon their return. It was this mass exodus prior to the 1948 War of Independence and again in 1967 that led in part to the Palestinian problem. After Israel soundly defeated the invading Arab countries, those Arabs who fled became referred to as "Palestinians" rather than the Jordanians, Egyptians, and Arabs that they truly were, and they have been trying to get the spoils of war they were promised ever since.

Islamic World Domination

Throughout Islam's long history, world domination has been its goal. The partial crescent moon that symbolizes the religion of Islam was to one day become a full moon. Muhammad prophesied that the Islamic Caliphate that ruled over the Ottoman Empire at the height of Islam's power would rise again in the last days. The Caliphate would once again be established over an Islamic world under the leadership of the Twelfth Imam, or Mahdi. The following Haddith explains this prophecy.

1. William Muir, *Life of Mahomet* (1876), p. 237.

The Prophet (peace be upon him) said, "Prophecy will remain among you as long as Allah wishes it to remain, then Allah Most High will remove it. Then there will be a caliphate according to the manner of prophecy as long as Allah wishes it to remain, then Allah Most High will remove it. Then there will be a distressful kingdom which will remain as long as Allah wishes it to remain, then Allah Most High will remove it. Then there will be a proud kingdom which will remain as long as Allah wishes it to remain, then Allah Most High will remove it. Then there will be a caliphate according to the manner of prophecy."[2]

Throughout Muhammad's writings there are striking similarities to the Bible. At times, he plagiarized entire sections of Scripture, and at other times, as in this case, he took an idea from the Christian Bible and altered it for his own purposes. In this Hadith, Muhammad twists the prophecies of Daniel that predict the rise of four world empires throughout history, and inserts the caliphate as two of those empires. Following the Islamic empire that rose to power as Rome's influence was declining, Muhammad prophesied that there would be a distressful kingdom, followed by a proud kingdom, and then the caliphate and Islamic power would once again be restored. The United States is seen among Muslims as being that proud empire that will be destroyed when the 12th imam returns. The Islamic world also sees the war on terror as the Third Great Jihad, and the goal in winning that war is a future global empire governed by Islamic law. The strategy of Islamic terrorist groups is first to eliminate moderate Islamic governments around the world, such as Musharif's Pakistan, the reigning monarchy in Saudi Arabia, and Egypt, who give the appearance of supporting the West. The West is fully aware of this, and it's for this reason that, following 9/11, they propped up the Pakistani government and are now fighting wars in Afghanistan and Iraq.

---

2. Al-Tirmidhi Hadith 53-78/Narrated by Al-Imâm Abu Haneefah An-Nu'man.

With Islam united they plan to destroy Israel, America, and other secular countries, in preparation for the Mahdi's return, and the fulfillment of Muhammad's prophecy concerning a final Islamic caliphate.

A war in the Middle East is going to break out, and I believe it's going to happen very soon. I believe that because, more than any other time in history, the world stage is set for just such a war. That war will be followed by the rise of the Antichrist and seven years of righteous judgment on the nations of the world.

We Live in a Prophetic Time

What makes our time different than other times in history? There are two key issues that make our generation different than any other. For the first time in over 1,900 years the Jews are back in their land and the nation of Israel is once again a Jewish homeland. When Israel became a state in 1948, the end times began, and we have been drawing ever closer to the final seven years in history ever since. For decades now the Jews have been returning home to the nation of Israel. The Lord said in Ezekiel 37:21, "I will take the Israelites out of the nations where they have gone. I will gather them from all around and bring them back into their own land." During the years from 1948 to 1967, over 600,000 Jews returned to Israel from surrounding Islamic countries alone. From 1967 to 1998, nearly 200 new Jewish settlements were established within Israel, and thousands of Jews continue to return to their homeland each year.[3] The prophesied return of the Jews to Israel has been fulfilled in the end times and the desert has blossomed once again, just as God said it would. Ezekiel 38 tells us that when the Jews have returned to their homeland, the next prophetic event in God's plan is an Islamic invasion of the re-gathered Jewish nation.

Our generation is also different because, for the first time in the history of the world, we have terrorist nations in possession,

---

3. Randall Price, *Fast Facts on the Middle East Conflict* (Eugene, OR: Harvest House Publishers, 2003), p. 130.

or in the process of acquiring, nuclear weapons. Nuclear weapons in the hands of countries like Iran and North Korea, or given to terrorist groups by a country like Pakistan or Russia, makes our generation uniquely qualified to witness the kind of carnage and utter destruction described in Ezekiel 38.

The Three Fronts of Radical Islam

Islamic terrorism itself also sets our time apart from others, and signals the nearness of Christ's return for His Church, and a coming war in the Middle East. Radical Islam is waging the third and final jihad on three fronts in our world today. The first front can be seen most prominently in the words and actions of Iran's president, Mahmoud Ahmadinejad. A state-run website in Iran recently heralded the coming of Imam Mahdi, who disappeared in A.D. 941, noting that he could return by the spring equinox. "Imam Mahdi (may God hasten his reappearance) will appear all of a sudden on the world scene with a voice from the skies announcing his reappearance at the holy Ka'ba in Mecca," the message proclaimed.[4] The Islamic Republic of Iran Broadcasting website aired a program called "The World Toward Illumination" that told viewers "the Mahdi would form an army to defeat the enemies of Islam in a series of apocalyptic battles, in which the Mahdi will overcome his arch villain in Jerusalem."[5] Little do they know, there will only be one apocalyptic battle, and the Third Jihad will end on the mountains of Israel with their army's utter destruction at the hand of God.

Ahmadinejad has openly declared his intentions to the world, and threatened to wipe Israel from the map. For months he has been broadcasting to the world exactly what Iran is going to do, just as Hitler told us what his plans were for the world in 1938, but the world is infected with political correctness and wishful thinking. Politicians ignore reality and promise peace where there can be none, just to get elected, and our secular world blindly

4. "Iran Website Heralding 'Mahdi' by Spring," Worldnet Daily, 2006, http://www.worldnetdaily.com/news/article.asp?ARTICLE_ID=53577.
5. http://www.6000years.org/articles/iran_mahdi.html, 2006.

follows and ignores the threats from our enemies' own mouths. It is for this reason that the war on terror will never end. We can't defeat an enemy we deny even exists, and we can't prevent a regional war fought because of Islam's desire to dominate the world, if we continue to pretend Islam is a religion of peace. Because the world ignores Islam's long history of conquest and slaughter, choosing instead to blame cultural insensitivity or political bungling, they will see Islam's history repeated with the same disastrous consequences.

The threat to Israel of a war with Iran and the other Arab countries that surround her, already exists, and continues to grow. The "National Council of Resistance of Iran" (NCRI), an Iranian opposition group that first exposed Iran's nuclear program, and has been seeking to overthrow the current regime in Iran since the 80s, recently gave the United Nations nuclear watchdog, the International Atomic Energy Agency (IAEA), details, including satellite imagery, of what they claim is a nuclear warhead development facility in Iran. Mohammad Mohaddessin, the foreign affairs chief for the group, reported that a facility in Khojir is being used to develop a nuclear warhead compatible with Iranian medium-range missiles. They also claim that houses near the facility are being occupied by nuclear specialists from North Korea who are passing on North Korea's nuclear technology, and helping the Iranians with the complex uranium enrichment process needed to build an atomic weapon.

The NCRI has given accurate and verifiable information to the IAEA twice in the past. In both cases the intelligence was later confirmed by inspectors, lending credibility to the group's claims. Their efforts to locate the facility in Iran are a direct response to the 2007 United States National Intelligence Estimate (NIE) that concluded Iran halted its nuclear weapons program in 2003. The NIE did a great deal to reduce American support for dealing with Iran's nuclear program, and the NCRI is eager to prove to the international community and the United States that the nuclear threat from Iran is still a very real and eminent danger to the world.

Iran's nuclear program, in conjunction with their North Korean based Shahab3 missile, poses a very dangerous threat to the nation of Israel. Designed after North Korea's Nodong1 missile, the Shahab3 can reach as far as 1,240 miles, putting Israel within range of an Iranian nuclear attack, should they acquire a warhead or succeed in producing their own.[6]

When the NIE was made public by the United States Intelligence community, Israel was quick to tell the United States that they had intelligence that proved Iran was still moving forward with their nuclear weapons program. As is usually the case when Israeli leaders speak up in defense of the Jewish nation, their claims were dismissed and the media continued to focus on the National Intelligence Estimate. The NIE contained the information they wanted to hear, and the accusations that President Bush was simply trying to start another war based on inaccurate intelligence have been trumpeted from our mainstream media ever since its release.

Israel, however, is not going to stick its collective head in the sand and ignore a threat that could potentially bring about the destruction of Israel that Iran's president has been promising.

In 2008, Muhammad Ali Jafari, the commander of Iran's Revolutionary Guard, promised that the day was rapidly approaching when Hezbullah would achieve its goal of destroying Israel. In addition to threats from terrorist groups in the Middle East, Iran has stepped up its rhetoric and threats of destroying Israel. Since the assassination of Imad Muhgniyeh, a senior Hezbullah leader in Damascus in 2008, Iran's threats have become increasingly belligerent, and are seen by Israel as indicating serious intent by the nation's leaders. Israel's Chief of Staff, Lt. General Gaby Ashkenazi, warned in a speech that he could not rule out a possible "tough ordeal" with Iran in the near future.[7]

Adding to the threat from Iran is the increasingly hostile tone from surrounding Arab nations who have, until recently, stayed out of the recent war of words from Iran, because of their oil ties to the West, and

---

6. Marc Champion, "Exile Group Claims Iran is Developing Nuclear Warheads," *Wall Street Journal*, February 20, 2008.
7. Hana Levi Julian, "Abbas Nixes PA Declaration of Statehood," February 20, 2008, http://www.israelnationalnews.com.

their need for foreign aid. For example, as the debate over the division of Jerusalem and the creation of a Palestinian state was heating up in early 2008, Saudi Arabia's foreign minister hinted in statements to the media that Arab countries might take back their peace offers to Israel, if they do not agree to hand over East Jerusalem to the Palestinians in a final Middle East peace agreement.[8]

Radical Islam's Second Front

Islam's second front in their war against civilization and the rest of the civilized world is a matter of procreation, population growth, and suicide. Women in the Islamic world don't have careers, they have children — usually six or more. Without detonating a single suicide bomb or launching an attack, Islam is defeating the West by slowly becoming a majority. Not only is Islam experiencing a population explosion, it's the fastest-growing religion in the world. Giving people the choice of converting or facing death will do that for a religion. There are over one billion Muslims in the world, and millions of them are willing to die for their faith. Muslim mothers have babies, and hope that they will grow up to become a martyr for Allah. In contrast, American women have abortions and hope for a better career and more money. That's why countries like France, Britain, Holland, and others are beginning to complain of a hostile takeover of their culture by expanding Muslim communities. In fact, Europe is becoming known as Eurabia as the Muslim numbers climb. As long as it's politically incorrect to restrict immigration, and mothers in the West routinely kill their babies, Muslim influence will only continue to grow around the world.

Radical Islam's Third Front

The third front in Islam's war on the West is economic in nature. Arab countries have the power to destroy America economically, if they can do so in a united way, and with the help of other nations. As we'll explore further in chapter 8, Iran is currently working to change the way oil is purchased around the world. All

8. Ibid.

oil is currently purchased using U.S. dollars. This necessitates the stockpiling of U.S. currency by every country that purchases oil from countries like Iran. This, in turn, strengthens the U.S. dollar, and greatly affects America's economy. Since Iran has accomplished replacing the U.S. dollar with the euro and other currencies in all oil sales transactions. This will mean far-reaching consequences for the United States economy, and will affect every one of our lives. In essence, Iran will have brought the Arab world a giant step closer to their goal of destroying the only superpower left in the world, and shifting the balance of power to Europe and the Arab world.

The End of the Church Age

In Matthew 24, Jesus Himself gave us several signs that would mark the end of the Church Age. In verse 2, as Jesus and the disciples surveyed the Temple buildings from the mountains around Jerusalem, He told them that we would know the end of the age had arrived when there was not one building or wall left standing on the Temple Mount. If you'll recall, we learned in Ezekiel 38 that God would use a powerful earthquake to inflict punishment on the allied Islamic forces who will invade Israel in the last days. It stands to reason that this earthquake will fulfill the prophesied destruction of every structure on the Temple Mount. As we'll cover later, this may also bring about the destruction of the Dome of the Rock, and pave the way for the rebuilding of the Jewish Temple. I believe we may, or may not, be here to witness this sign of the end of the age. The Rapture will take place either right before, or during the aftermath of the invasion of Israel, but we don't know exactly when the Lord will return. That's part of the beauty of God's plan. His return can't be predicted with exact certainty, so we must live as if Christ could return today.

The next end-times sign Jesus gives the disciples is in the form of a warning. He told them not to be deceived by many who will come in Jesus' name, claiming to be the returning Messiah. This has certainly been fulfilled in our time. There is no shortage of prophets, christs, and saviors claiming to be the returned messiah, and they have a surprising number of faithful followers willing to believe them. A Florida man named Jose Luis de Jesus Miranda founded Growing in Grace International Ministry after having a dream and, he claims, integrating with Christ Himself. He presides over a sprawling organization that includes more than 300 congregations in two dozen countries, from Argentina to Australia. He counts more than 100,000 followers and claims to reach millions more through a 24-hour TV channel, a radio show, and several websites. His followers have donated millions of dollars to the cause, providing an extravagant lifestyle for Miranda, complete with fancy cars and extravagant jewelry. His faithful have no problem with the fact that Miranda first claimed to be the Apostle Paul before claiming to be Jesus Christ, and, changing his story once again, now claims to be the Antichrist, complete with the mark of the Beast tattooed on his arm.

There are many Miranda's around the world, and just as Jesus prophesied, they have deceived many. It saddens me to hear of so many people who are so completely ignorant of the teachings of the Bible as to be taken advantage of by a man claiming to be their Savior. Our churches can be partly to blame for this. Too many pastors pass over end-times prophecy in their sermons, believing their congregations don't want to hear about doom and gloom, and the destruction of the wicked. Likewise, too many Christians only want to hear warm and fuzzy sermons that make them feel good about themselves, whether they are living a Christ-centered life or not. As a result, people are not hearing the whole truth in their churches. Christians are unprepared to answer books like *The Da Vinci Code* and *The Shack,* as well as refute heresy like the Emergent Church movement. Many believers are being deceived by fine-sounding arguments and doctrines taught by demons. This deception within the Church is on the rise, and it also signals the nearness of Christ's return.

Jesus also tells us in Matthew 24 that the end times will see nation rise against nation. In other words, there will be a dramatic increase in ethnic wars around the world. In our world today there are at least 70 different ethnic clashes taking place. Radical Islamic groups are waging jihad and engaging in ethnic cleansing across Africa and around the world. Throughout the Middle East Muslims are revising history, and executing land grabs that leave thousands homeless and penniless (if they escape with their lives at all). A map found on a Palestinian website shows the tiny nation of Israel surrounded by millions of square miles of Arab land, and the caption reads "end the unjust occupation of the Arab land." Insane arguments like this have actually gained backing by a large majority of people and nations, and are accepted as a legitimate excuse for terrorism and the slaughter of innocent civilians. As a result, there has been an escalation in the frequency of these conflicts. This escalation is the third thing Jesus warns us will take place in the last days, just before the Tribulation.

The increase in wars, deception, and suffering around the world as we near a time of even greater chaos can be depressing, but it shouldn't be. Jesus didn't give us these signs, or the signs we will cover in future chapters, to scare us. He didn't intend for us to dwell on death and destruction, or live in fear, but to be watchful and look forward to His return. In other words, these prophecies weren't given to scare us, but to prepare us. In verse 6, Jesus tells us not to be alarmed when we see these events taking place. As believers, our salvation is secure, and while we may witness some of these signs as we approach the End of Days, we were not appointed to suffer through God's wrath and judgment on this wicked world. We should be prepared, keep watch, and warn our friends and loved ones that time is running out, but we can also feel excitement and joy that our time on this earth is limited. Something so much better awaits us when Christ returns to take His Church out of the way, and complete God's perfect plan for us.

Chapter 5

THE GREAT DECEIVER

Have you ever been talking with someone and as you were speaking, he or she stared at you with a blank look that reminded you of a deer caught in the headlights? This seems to be the response from most people when they hear about this sinister character spoken of in the Bible called the Antichrist. Is there really such a person or is this a myth? If there is such a character, who or what is he and when will we know?

The writers of the best-selling Left Behind series call him Nicolae. He is tall, handsome, wealthy, and thirsty for power. He is portrayed as the ultimate human being but without real feelings and heartfelt compassion and he rules the post-Rapture world. After *Left Behind*, additional books in the series followed with such intriguing titles as *Desecration, The Mark, The Indwelling, The Rising*, and lastly *The Regime*. The very idea of a world ruler called the Antichrist has infatuated Hollywood for many years. Producer Don Taylor called him Damien in the movies *Omen* in 1976 and *Omen II* in '78, and portrayed his dark and evil side as he learns who he really is. Could such a diabolical personality really exist or is he only a figment of Hollywood's mind?

Satan worship has grown at an alarming rate in America in recent years and the tattoo industry along with it. It is common to see tattoos portraying the numbers "666," a symbol associated with the Antichrist on the bodies of America's youth. What is this all about? Is it fact or fiction? Let's find out!

Following the devastation and utter destruction wrought by the Islamic invasion of Israel, and the resulting destruction of the Islamic countries, the nations of the world will be ready to make unthinkable concessions. They will surrender their national sovereignty and loyalty, along with their long cherished rights, in submission to a powerful and persuasive leader who will promise them peace and safety. In a world turned on end by the departure of the Church, and the indescribable carnage in Israel, the Antichrist will arrive on the scene to deceive the masses with the Great Lie and the promise of peace.

As David Rockefeller of the Trilateral Commission and the Council on Foreign Relations once said, "We are on the verge of a global transformation. All we need is the right major crisis and the nations will accept the New World Order."[1] Many of our leaders have already expressed their willingness to give up our national sovereignty in response to a global crisis, war, or any threat to world peace. George Bush Sr. said of the Gulf War in 1990, "The Persian Gulf crisis is a rare opportunity to forge new bonds with old enemies. Out of these troubled times a New World Order can emerge under a United Nations that performs as envisioned by its founders."[2] How much more eager will these leaders be to give up our sovereignty and freedoms to this fraud when faced with the vanishing of millions of their citizens, and the utter destruction of the oil-producing Arab countries of the world? This set of circumstances, coupled with the Antichrist's powers of deception and intrigue, will convince those who rule

1. David Rockefeller, speaking at the UN, Sept. 14, 1994, http://www. newswithviews.com/BeritKjos/kjos60.htm.
2. President H.W. Bush addressing Congress, September 11, 1990, http://www. newswithviews.com/BeritKjos/kjos60.htm.

over us to do things we never would have dreamed they would do in a pre-Rapture world.

Before we begin our study of the Antichrist, I want to reiterate that those of us who have put our faith in Jesus Christ prior to the Rapture of the Church will not be here for any of the events we will be discussing from this point forward. True believers will not see the invasion of Israel, and will never know who the Antichrist is, because he will arrive on the scene after we have been translated into heaven in the Rapture.

The Rapture of millions of believers will change everything, and affect every life that remains on this planet. Following the Rapture and God's punishment on those who will invade Israel, a rapid succession of events will take place around the globe. There will be drastic changes that we can't even imagine being possible as the world tries to pull itself up from chaos, and people begin the process of restoring some sense of order and normalcy to their lives. Among those events will be the rise of a world leader who will deceive the world with a great lie. The lie this personality will espouse will attempt to explain away the vanishing of millions, while attempting to lure those remaining into a false sense of safety and hope.

Who Is the Antichrist Going to Be?

In recent years, there has been a great amount of discussion about who the Antichrist is, or will be. Hollywood has been obsessed with this diabolical ruler, which is truly ironic since Hollywood is equally obsessed with mocking Christianity and taunting Christians for their belief in end-times prophecy.

When it comes to identifying the Antichrist, everyone from Barack Obama to Bill Clinton to Mikhail Gorbachev has been a suspect at one time or another. These join the likes of Prince Philip of Spain as well as Ronald Reagan and even Al Gore! At every prophecy conference I am part of, there is always at least one person among the crowd who will approach me and claim to have figured out who the Antichrist is. They'll tell me in all sincerity that they've unraveled the mystery, and can, without a doubt, identify the man who will usher in the seven-year Tribulation. It might be anyone from their next door neighbor, to their micro-managing boss, to Bill and/or Hillary Clinton, and nowadays, Barack Obama. Whenever someone shares one of these dramatic revelations with me, I instinctively grab my wallet. I figure if someone will lie like that, they'll probably steal, too. The truth is, we believers will never know his identity. The Apostle Paul gives us important information about the Antichrist in the second chapter of his second letter to the Thessalonians. He instructs us that our departure will allow the Antichrist to reveal himself.

However, while pre-Rapture Christians can never know his identity, Jesus did instruct us to be aware of the signs of the times, and be ready. It is for this reason that we should be aware of what the Bible reveals about this coming ruler. If we know what kind of man he will be, and what he will do when he arrives, we will also be able to recognize the signs that his arrival is near, and prepare ourselves and our loved ones for Christ's return.

The Bible's Answer to Who the Antichrist Is

To understand who the Antichrist is, we first need to look again at Daniel chapter 7. As was covered earlier, Daniel's dream of four beasts represents four world empires that would rule on the earth from Daniel's time until Christ's return. In verse 7, Daniel records that this fourth beast, or world empire, will be different from the previous three. It will be exceedingly terrifying, awesome, and strong, and it will have ten horns. In Daniel chapter 2, we're given more information about this empire. Verse 40 says that it will be strong, yet mixed. This diverse empire will be divided as represented by the potters clay and iron that make up the statue's feet in Nebuchadnezzar's dream of four future world empires, but it will also be strong like the fourth beast's large iron teeth. We're also told in Daniel chapter 7 that a small horn will rise up among the ten horns and uproot three of them. This smaller horn in Daniel's dream has eyes like a man, and is seen speaking haughty, boastful words. Before we discuss this smaller horn and the meaning of the ten-horned empire of Daniel's vision, we can gather further information about this final beast and the little horn from John's Revelation.

Revelation chapter 13 similarly describes a beast with ten horns, but we're also given the identity of the little horn that will arise and speak haughty words. The little horn is none other than the Antichrist, and Satan himself will give this future ruler his power and throne, as well as great authority on earth to carry out Satan's assault on God's creation.

Revelation 13:11 says, "Then I saw another beast, coming out of the earth. He had two horns like a lamb, but he spoke like a dragon." The future ruler of the fourth and final world empire is given many names in the Bible. He's called the man of sin and the son of perdition in 2 Thessalonians, and in 1 John 2:18 he is referred to as the Antichrist. First John is the only book in the New Testament to refer to this tool of Satan as the Antichrist. The name itself and its meaning are important to our study. John recorded at the end of the first century that many Antichrists had already come, and they would continue to appear and deceive many people throughout the church age. But, as we read John's account of the church age and the end times, we learn that these antichrists are precursors to a final satanic masterpiece. These false christs foreshadow the coming of a final incarnation of human evil that will arrogate for himself a position of power over the entire earth.

First John 2:18 further warns, "Dear children, this is the last hour; and as you have heard that the antichrist is coming, even now many antichrists have come. This is how we know it is the last hour." This teaching of a final imposter who will establish himself as the returning Christ, complete with an unholy trinity mimicking the true triune God, was rooted in the earliest Christian teaching. Even the Jews had long taught that there would be a future anti-Messiah, who in Jewish lore was called Armilus. Christian references to a final anti-Messiah in the last days can be found in some of the earliest Christian writings, such as the Apocalypse of Peter, the Didache, the Pseudo-Titus Epistle, and in the writings of various church fathers.

The Greek prefix *anti* in this verse can be defined as "opposed to," or "a substitute for." The Antichrist will be a substitute for the real Christ and against Christ at the same time. Everything he does will be designed to support the claim the he is Jesus Christ returned.

I believe this final imposter is alive today. Our amoral, depraved world is more ready for the deception of just such a leader than at any time in history. Somewhere in the world today, this embodiment of evil and his false prophet are waiting in the wings for the right time to step onto the world stage and offer the answer to a desperate people in a time of utter chaos and confusion. Sadly, they are totally unaware of the role they will play in the future!

Daniel's dream of four beasts is important because it's telling us what is going to happen in the end times, after the Rapture. In both the dream of the four beasts and the statue with four distinct parts, the final world empire is described as having ten horns, or ten kings. When the Antichrist is unveiled, he will subdue three of the ten kings. Indwelt by Satan, he will deceive the world with the great lie that he is God, sign a peace treaty with Israel, and begin what will be a seven-year tyrannical rule over the earth.

In chapter 2 of Daniel, we saw these same four future world empires described in the interpretations of Nebuchadnezzar's dream of a great statue. As we will cover in more detail later, this final kingdom that will give birth to the Antichrist's rise to power is already being set up with the formation of the European Union (E.U). The E.U. exists as a ten-nation confederacy, with the original ten nations holding permanent member status and the subsequently joining nations holding only observer status, fitting perfectly with the description of the fourth beast in Daniel. We will also see in later chapters that the United Nations has already divided the globe into ten bioregions, paving the way for the future political system that will be established under the leadership of the Antichrist.

Four Goals of E.U. Defense Agency

• Develop defense capabilities

• Promote defense research/technology

• Promote armaments cooperation

• Create competitive tech/industrial base

These two dreams give us a composite picture of what the world political system, ruled over by the Antichrist for seven years, will look like. Elsewhere in Daniel, we're given several very specific facts that can help us understand in greater detail just who and what this man of evil will be. The first thing we can know with certainty is that the Antichrist will rise up from the revived form of the ancient Roman Empire. Daniel 9:25 says that, from the time of the issuing of the decree to restore and rebuild Jerusalem, until the Anointed One comes, there will be seven "sevens," and sixty-two "sevens." After sixty-two sevens, or 483 years, Daniel tells us that the Anointed One will be cut off and have nothing. This was fulfilled with the crucifixion of Christ exactly 483 years after the rebuilding of Jerusalem and the Jewish Temple, as it is partially narrated in Ezra and Nehemiah. We're told that after Christ's death and Resurrection, "the people of the ruler who will come" (Daniel 9:26) will destroy the city and the sanctuary. This prophecy was fulfilled in September of A.D. 70 when Rome, under Titus, destroyed Jerusalem. After a period of time, during which wars will continue to be fought, this ruler will "confirm a covenant with many for one seven." This 70th week that Daniel speaks of in verse 27 is a reference to the seven-year tribulation period that will take place after the church age and the Rapture. These verses provide key information about the Antichrist's identity. They tell us that he will come from the same people who destroyed Jerusalem in A.D. 70. The Roman Empire under Vespasian fulfilled this prophecy; therefore, we can surmise that the Antichrist will arise to power from within the Roman Empire, which in our time is the European Union. Remember, the Rapture changes everything! The E.U. as we know it today will be vastly different in the hours and days following the Rapture.

John's revelation gives us insight into the Antichrist's motives for establishing this global empire. Revelation 13 says that the Antichrist will speak like a dragon, but will have horns like a lamb. In other words, he will speak like Satan, but will appear to be Jesus, and the fulfillment of Christ's return. He will be an imposter, and will do everything he can including miracles, signs, and lying wonders to convince the world that he fulfills all of the messianic prophecies in the Bible, and those of all religions around the world. The Antichrist will be so eager to take Christ's place and rule over the earth in Christ's stead that he will even mimic the death and Resurrection of Christ.

Revelation 13:3 tells us that the Antichrist will seem to have received a fatal wound. Following this seemingly fatal wound he will be miraculously healed, astonishing the world, and convincing many that the he is worthy of their trust and, more importantly, their worship. People around the world will see this miraculous healing and resurrection, and unknowingly sell their souls to the devil to follow him.

Satan has always been the master of all liars and imposters. It has also always been his desire to be worshipped. In fact, it is for this reason that he took Jesus into the wilderness and offered Him everything as far as the eye could see in exchange for Jesus' worship and devotion. Satan has never lost that desire to be worshiped, and he wants more than anything to receive the worship that belongs only to Jesus Christ. During the Tribulation, he will try to imitate everything that Jesus did in His earthly ministry, including His death, burial, and Resurrection.

It's not uncommon for people to mistake this future ruler in Revelation 13 for Jesus, when He returns to reign over the Millennial Kingdom. However, we know this is not the case, because the future ruler spoken of in this passage will be one who causes desolation until the very end.

God's Prophetic Clock

God's prophetic clock stopped with the death, burial, and Resurrection of Christ and we have been in a sort of holding pattern for centuries. During these last roughly 2,000 years, believers have been fulfilling God's promise that the gospel message would be spread throughout the world. Jesus told the Apostles that there would be a period of time following His time on earth when people would travel here and there, increasing in knowledge, and fighting many wars and battles before the end would come. He was speaking of the church age, and that's exactly what has happened over the centuries since Christ's ascension into heaven. It would be during this time that God would raise up a new people called the Church to spread the Good News, and bring many to a saving relationship with Christ. At some time in the very near future, the Church's job will be finished, and we will be taken out of the way. At a time known only to the Father, somewhere in the world, someone will give his or her life to Christ and the Father will announce that the last one has been saved. He will then turn to Christ, and tell Him to go and get His Bride.

God's prophetic clock will resume ticking after the Rapture, when the Tribulation begins. I want to make sure this point is very clear. The beginning of the Tribulation is not the Rapture of the Church. Sometime after the Rapture, the Antichrist will enter into a peace agreement with Israel. However, there could be months, or even years, before such an agreement is made, and the seven years of wrath and judgment on earth begins. In fact, logic dictates that it will probably take some time for the world to recover from the chaos left behind after the Rapture. In addition, the world must recover from the Islamic invasion of Israel and come to grips with the world situation, unite behind the European Union, and come to know and appreciate the man who will promise them the peace and safety they long for. An agreement between the Antichrist and the nations to rebuild the Temple in Jerusalem will be reached at some point, and only then will the final seven years of God's plan unfold.

Between the Rapture and the Tribulation

Many things are going to take place in the period of time between the Rapture and the Tribulation. Remember, the Islamic invasion will also not likely take place until after the Church's departure. God will use this great slaughter and defeat of the Islamic world to bring Israel's enemies to the table and prepare them for the Antichrist's diplomatic solution. Faced with a humiliating defeat and the carnage wrought by the war, these countries will become willing participants in a treaty that makes concessions that would seem impossible in a pre-rapture world.

Daniel 11:36 says that the Antichrist will be successful in his political, economic, and global ambitions for the seven years that he is in power. However, this doesn't mean that Satan will be able to use the Antichrist to do his will on earth. God is in control of everything that happens in this world, and neither Satan nor the Antichrist can change God's plan. In other words, everything the Antichrist will be able to accomplish on this earth, as well as how much power and authority he receives, is predetermined by God. God's plan cannot be altered.

Daniel 11 also gives us a look into the Antichrist's motives, as well as the personality traits and spiritual beliefs that he will display as he deceives the world. Daniel 11:37 reads, "He will show no regard for the gods of his fathers or for the one desired by women, nor will he regard any god, but will exalt himself above them all."

The Antichrist will show no regard for Jesus, other than to mimic His life for the purposes of deceiving people, and he will have no interest or regard for the gods that have been worshiped in the past. In fact, he will claim to be superior to all of them. Much like Mohammed claimed to be a prophet of higher stature and status than Jesus, and countless other false prophets have claimed to be greater than their predecessors, the Antichrist will place himself above all others.

In addition to deception, diplomacy, and a promise of peace and safety, the Antichrist will rise to power by using the same tactics employed by politicians throughout history. He will offer his coat tails and a smooth ride to the top. Those who support him will be made rulers, given booty, and offered more power. Following him will hold many perks, but resisting him will come at a great price.

Daniel further writes in Daniel 11:40, what will happen to those nations who resist the Antichrist's rise to power. He will launch invasions, and in a great rage, annihilate any dissenters. Countries from China in the East, Russia in the North, and around the world will either side with the Antichrist, or they will fall to his armies.

Daniel 11:37 presents another possible characteristic of the Antichrist, but the meaning of this verse can be as much a matter of opinion as interpretation. The verse states that the Antichrist will hold no regard for the god desired by women. Some people interpret this to mean that the Antichrist will be homosexual, while others believe that this is a reference to the Babylonian fertility God Tammuz, which is mentioned in Ezekiel 8:14 as being worshiped by women in the Temple. This verse may very well indicate that the Antichrist will be homosexual, but with verses like this, it is important not to force Scripture to say something that it does not really say. There's a big difference between a preacher or Bible scholar's opinion, and what the Bible actually says. I happen to believe that there is a strong possibility that the Antichrist will indeed be homosexual. Homosexuality is an abomination and a sin of sexual immorality. Since the Antichrist will be the opposite of everything Jesus taught, and because he will be indwelt by the father of all lies, it makes sense that his sexuality would also be the evil flip side of what God created to be holy and natural. However, this is just my opinion. The Bible doesn't answer this question for us with any certainty. Opinion is no substitute for an uncompromising literal interpretation of Scripture.

You may be wondering how one man will convince the entire world to follow him and give him all power and authority over a global government. The fact is, the world has been waiting for just such a man for centuries. Throughout history, we see humanity's eagerness to throw their support and devotion behind a single personality who can lead them to the perfect utopia. Mankind has been striving to create that world ever since the first attempt to reach heaven without God, by building the Tower of Babel.

Uniting the World

Jack Lang, former president of the French National Assembly's foreign affairs committee said in a speech given in Paris, "The E.U. needs a strong central government with a single personality at the helm."[3] The United Nations has long championed the need for a global system of government. We will reveal in chapter 6 a spiritual agenda of sorts at the United Nations that expects and eagerly awaits the appearance of a single man. This man will be a kind of savior who will unite the world under a government that fulfills their mission as laid out in the U.N. charter.

Paul Henry Spaak, secretary general of the United Nations from 1957–1961 once said, "We do not want another committee, we have too many already. What we want is a man of sufficient stature to hold the allegiance of all people, and to lift us out of the economic morass in which we are sinking." He continued, "Send us such a man, and be he god or devil, we will receive him."[4]

Even in the United States, the last holdout against socialist humanism, there is a strong globalist movement that has infiltrated the halls of Congress and the U.S. presidency. President George Bush Sr. said in his 1991 State of the Union Address, "The world can therefore seize the opportunity (the Persian Gulf war) to fulfill the long held promise of a New World Order, where diverse nations are drawn together in common cause to achieve the universal aspirations of mankind." How much more of an opportunity would something as devastating as the Rapture and the Islamic invasion of Israel and the subsequent mass slaughter of those Islamic countries be to those who envision a New World Order in our future. It will

---

3. *The London Times*, August 19, 1997, quoting a speech given by Jack Lang in Paris.
4. http://www.angelfire.com/realm/ofstardust/RISE_AC.html.

indeed draw diverse nations, represented by a mixture of iron and clay in Bible prophecy, together in a common cause.

Unlike the true God of the universe, Satan does not know when the Rapture will occur, or who the Antichrist will be. That's why, in every generation, there has been a leader who tried to reach the prophetic goal of establishing a new world order with one leader at the helm. Throughout history there have been personalities who have deceived millions, slaughtered innocents, and attempted to fulfill Satan's evil desire to conquer the world for evil. Men like Hitler, Stalin, and even Iran's current President Ahmadinejad have been sent over and over again by Satan to deceive the world. Very soon, one man will succeed.

Five Ways to Identify the Antichrist

There are five specific facts given to us in Scripture that will allow those who are not deceived by his cunning lie to identify this future ruler as the Antichrist. While those of us who believe in Christ, and are raptured prior to the Antichrist's appearance will never know who this man is, we can see the groundwork being laid for his arrival. Tribulation Saints (those who accept Christ after the Rapture) will be able to know without a doubt who the Antichrist really is.

First, as was covered earlier, he will rise to power out of the revived form of the old Roman Empire, which is now in existence as the European Union. Second, he will come to power sometime after the Rapture of the Church, and will enter into a seven-year covenant with Israel that will lead to the rebuilding of the Temple and the resumption of the Jewish sacrificial system.

Third, the Bible gives specifics with regard as to how the Antichrist will rise to power. Daniel 8:24–25 tells us that he will come to power through deception. He will be a master of intrigue, elevating himself above God, and he will offer peace and security to a war-torn world. All of his diplomatic efforts will succeed, because, as Daniel 7:20 says, he will be an intelligent man with unique powers of persuasion. In other words, he will be the consummate politician, able to rule with near unanimous international consent (Revelation 17:12–13).

People of every nation will join their leaders in consenting to the Antichrist's global ambitions, because he will be all things to all people. He will be the Mahdi to Muslims, the next reincarnation of Jesus to the Bah'ai, and the Maitreya to followers of the New Age Movement. To those who call themselves Christian, but were judged to be otherwise when the Church was raptured, he will be the Christ. Every religion that has been waiting for a messiah to come will see him as the answer to their cries for help, and the completion of an evolutionary plan for our world, ending in the utopist dream of so many cults, religions, and political movements around the world.

The fourth identifying characteristic will be the timing of his rise to power. He will not reveal himself, or his deceptive plan, until after the departure of the Church. In 2 Thessalonians, Paul says that while the power of lawlessness is already at work, the Lawless one, or Antichrist, will not be revealed until the one who restrains is taken out of the way. It is the presence of the Holy Spirit in the hearts of every believer that prevents Satan's evil scheme from being carried out now.

Lastly, we are told how he will be able to rule over the entire world. His global, political, and economic system will be most likely be implemented by the use of technology. Only in our generation has the technology been available for one man to control the economy of the entire world. As we will explore in the next chapter, the Antichrist will have at his disposal a host of technological marvels like radio frequency identifiers, smart cards, and biochip implants. Perhaps most importantly, he will have an economy that is already based on a global market and international trade agreements, as well as an interconnected banking system. As Henry Kissinger once said of free trade, "The North American Free Trade Agreement (NAFTA) is a major stepping stone to the New World Order."[5]

---

5. Los Angeles Times Syndicate, 1993.

Those who once rejected technology that posed a threat to their privacy and personal freedoms will submit to his authority in the name of security. A recent survey done in Europe revealed that 77 percent of the British people are willing to give up their individual freedoms in order to gain security and protection from terrorist attacks. Since 9/11, Americans have continued to aggressively relinquish long-cherished personal freedoms and rights to privacy in exchange for peace of mind, and protection from further terrorist attacks against the homeland. On January 20, 2005, famed ABC anchor Peter Jennings aired his documentary entitled, "No Place to Hide." Jennings stated, "People have a right to privacy but not anonymity." He went on to say that information mining is taking place 24/7 and that no one truly can grasp the depth of information about himself or herself that is available. His summary was, "If they want to find you, they will!" As I pondered the message of this enlightening program, the thought that came to my mind was, you can run but you cannot hide!

In March of 1993, Bill Clinton told *USA Today*, "We can't be so fixated on our desire to preserve the rights of ordinary Americans." H.L. Menchen, a prominent journalist and political commentator in the early 1900s may have said it best when he said, "The whole aim of practical politics is to keep the populace alarmed — and hence clamorous to be led to safety — and menacing it with an endless series of hobgoblins, all of them imaginary."[6]

Jimmy Carter's National Security Advisor, Zbigniew Brzezinski, said, "This regionalization of the world is in keeping with the Trilateral Plan which calls for a gradual convergence of East and West, ultimately leading toward the goal of one world government. National sovereignty is no longer a viable concept."[7] When the Antichrist emerges after the Rapture, the world will be more ready than ever before to accept a united world led by a powerful world ruler. When America's economy is devastated by the disappearance

---

6. http://www.brainyquote.com/quotes/quotes/h/hlmencke101109.html.
7. http://www.ontopofacloud.com/newworldorder.htm.

of millions of Americans, she will return to her roots and look to Europe for leadership. In future chapters, we will learn of the political and economic system that has already been established in the European Union and only awaits the right man to lead the world down a path to destruction.

The technology is already available to institute this global system of tyranny and enslavement. Thomas Jefferson, one of America's most quoted founding fathers, knew too well what our government was capable of without a series of checks and balances to keep politicians from usurping power that did not belong to them. When our country was just being born, he warned, "Single acts of tyranny may be ascribed to the accidental opinion of a day. But a series of oppressions, begun at a distinguished period, and pursued unalterably through every change of ministers, too plainly proves a deliberate systematic plan of reducing us to slavery."[8] This plan is being carried out and awaits only a man of sufficient stature and cunning to bring the world together behind its final goal. That man is coming soon. Thank God, we as believers will not be here to witness the judgment he will bring on the world through his satanic, global peace treaty.

Hollywood's darkest and most sinister writers cannot even begin to conjure up what this man will ultimately do as millions either commit to follow him or die!

---

8 http://thinkexist.com/quotation/single-acts-of-tyranny-may-be-ascribed-to-the/761253.html.

Chapter 6

GLOBAL RELIGION

What you are about to read may initially shock you. Please continue to read and know that my purpose is not to offend but to inform. This book is about truth and a warning of what is and will be.

One of the seven angels who had the seven bowls came and said to me, "Come, I will show you the punishment of the great prostitute, who sits on many waters. With her the kings of the earth committed adultery and the inhabitants of the earth were intoxicated with the wine of her adulteries." Then the angel carried me away in the Spirit into a desert. There I saw a woman sitting on a scarlet beast that was covered with blasphemous names and had seven heads and ten horns. The woman was dressed in purple and scarlet, and was glittering with gold, precious stones and pearls. She held a golden cup in her hand, filled with abominable things and the filth of her adulteries. This title was written on her forehead:

MYSTERY BABYLON THE GREAT
THE MOTHER OF PROSTITUTES
AND OF THE ABOMINATIONS OF THE EARTH.

I saw that the woman was drunk with the blood of the saints, the blood of those who bore testimony to Jesus (Revelation 17:1–6).

The Lust for Power

". . . working on issues of crime and education and employment and seeing that in some ways certain portions of the African American community are doing as bad if not worse, and recognizing that my fate remain tied up with their fates, that my individual salvation is not going to come about without a collective salvation for the country. Unfortunately, I think that recognition requires that we make sacrifices and this country has not always been willing to make the sacrifices that are necessary to bring about a new day and a new age."

President Barack Obama, July 13, 2010[1]

The European Union is now uniting politically, economically, and militarily. This unity will be needed to enforce the global laws of the Antichrist, and to eliminate dissenters during the Tribulation, but religious unity will play perhaps an even more critical part of the Antichrist's strategy for controlling the inhabitants of the earth.

Human beings have always had a thirst for something greater than themselves; something that will answer the great questions of life, and give their lives purpose beyond just living, evolving, and then simply ceasing to exist. Even in the very beginning of our existence on this planet, as recorded in the Book of Genesis, humans have been trying to substitute a man-made religion for the one true God. In Genesis 11, the inhabitants of the earth began to build a tower to the heavens in an attempt to reach God by themselves. They reasoned that they didn't need God's laws, and could use their own knowledge and ingenuity to reach the heavenly realms. Satan used the same lie to convince Eve that she could become like God

---

1. http://www.scribd.com/doc/71420207/Obama-Transcript.

by simply eating from the tree of knowledge, and he's been leading people astray ever since, by convincing them that they can attain godhood by their own will, instead of God's.

The Tower of Babel, built by a rebellious people, is the first appearance of the mystery religions of Babylon, and, as with the first appearance of sin in the Garden of Eden, it was dealt with harshly by God. He saved them from themselves by confusing their languages and scattering them across the earth. The word used in chapter 11 for the tower they attempted to build is Babel, which is the Hebrew word for Babylon. From this point forward the mystery religions of Babylon permeated the ancient world. They continued through the wife of Nimrod, who headed up another mystery religion in Babylon, the city founded by her husband. The influence of these pagan beliefs were incorporated into religious rights and ceremonies around the world, one of the most common being the belief in a queen of heaven. The Babylonian religions represent the first attempt to substitute an imitation for that which is real, and its influence can still be seen in many of the rituals and ceremonies of the Catholic Church. It's a wholly pagan idea to glorify and worship Mary, the mother of Jesus, as the Catholic Church does. It is this same pagan belief that Ezekiel protested in Ezekiel 8:5–14, and that led Jeremiah to object to the heathen practice of offering cakes and burning incense to Semirmis as the queen of heaven (Jeremiah 7:18).[2]

Ecumenical Views of the Roman Catholic Church

A man-made religion that seems to answer the right questions, while requiring nothing more than an acceptance of all beliefs, gods, and ideologies as equally valid has long been the goal of ecumenical religious systems and churches throughout the centuries perhaps, never more so than today. One church in particular has pursued this kind of religious unity with renewed vigor over the

2. John F. Walvoord, *Every Prophecy of the Bible* (Colorado Springs, CO: Chariot Victor Publishing, 1999), p. 605.

last decade. Unity at any cost is the new evangelism of the Roman Catholic Church and the Vatican. With the pope leading the way, the Vatican has launched numerous programs to bring together the great religions of the world under one set of guiding principles, all based on tolerance and acceptance, rather than truth and the Word of God. Since the second Ecumenical Council of the Vatican (Vatican II), the Catholic church has been building inroads and partnerships with world religions of every stripe and color, no matter how diametrically opposed they might be to the teachings of Christianity, and the Bible. Their goal is not so much to unite a diverse set of independent beliefs, but to bring the world's religions under the guidance and leadership of the pope. With the death of Pope John Paul, we saw just how universally revered the papacy has remained through the centuries, even among the media and unbelievers. National news channels, like Fox News, had wall-to-wall coverage of the pope's funeral ceremonies for weeks. They covered every detail of the new pope's selection, as well as the grandiose papal ceremonies that marked the beginning of Pope Benedict's papacy. Benedict was selected in large part based on his agreement with the views of Pope John Paul II, and a certainty that he would continue the ecumenical evangelism of the new century. Just as did his predecessor, the new pope has extended an olive branch to Muslims, Hindus, Buddhists, and even the New Age religions, which have made environmentalism more of a religion based on earth worship than a political movement.

In a 2008 visit to the United States, Pope Benedict addressed an interfaith gathering of more than 150 religious leaders, including leaders from the Hindu, Buddhist, Jain, Jewish, and Islamic religions. Representing the six to eight million Muslims in the United States was the national director of the Islamic Society of North America, Dr. Sayyid Syeed, who said recently that Catholics and Muslims have a particularly special relationship among the world religions. Evidence of this blossoming relationship between the Catholic Church and Islamic leaders can be seen in an agreement reached

between the two faiths in March of 2008 that committed both
religions to working together in a permanent official dialog to
improve relations and heal the wounds of the past.[3]

During the pope's speech before religious leaders who had
gathered in Washington DC for the April 2008 interfaith conference,
Jesus Christ was mentioned only once. Pope Benedict told the
audience that, when faced with the deeper questions concerning
the origin and destiny of mankind, Christianity proposes Jesus of
Nazareth. "He," the Pope announced, "we believe, is the eternal
Logos who became flesh in order to reconcile man to God and
reveal the underlying reason of all things."[4] While this may sound
like an effort to spread the gospel, I must point out that the pope
refers to Christ in terms of what Christians believe, rather than what
is the one and only truth for this world. While Christians propose
Christ as the only path to salvation, to the interfaith movement,
He remains an optional path to heaven, and just one of many. The
rest of his speech emphasized the Catholic Church's goal to unify
the religions of the world based on our common ethical values, and
common pursuit of peace in the world. It is a fact that you cannot
unify that which is contradictory without someone compromising
or accepting an opposing view as equally valid and true. It is this
kind of compromise that has watered down and rendered ineffective
the truth of the Bible among denominations that support the
interfaith movement. Christ cannot be the only path to salvation,
and Muhammad the only path to salvation, as the Muslims believe,
at the same time. Pope Benedict's reluctance to present Jesus Christ
as the only path to salvation can perhaps be explained by his 1964
sermon titled "Are Non-Christians Saved?" Benedict's answer to
that question is "yes." Not only can they be saved, but they can do
so without even knowing it. In his sermon he stated the following:

---

3. "Muslims, Vatican to Establish Permanent Dialogue," March 5,2008, http://
   www.dawn.com/2008/03/ 06/int10.htm.
4. "Pope to Host Interfaith Gathering During Visit to Washington," VOA News,
   04/08/2008, http://voanews.com/english/20080408voa22.cfm.

We are no longer ready, no longer willing, to think that eternal corruption should be inflicted on people in Asia, in Africa, or wherever it may be, merely on account of their not having "Catholic" marked in their passport.

Actually, a great deal of thought had been devoted in theology, both before and after Ignatius, to the question of how people, without even knowing it, in some way belonged to the Church and to Christ and could thus be saved nevertheless.

Instead of basing a person's eternal salvation on their belief in Christ, Pope Benedict instead approaches salvation much the same way the secular world does — as the result of one's adherence to a moral code, rather than the truth of what they believe. In other words, he falls for Satan's well used lie that says, anyone who can claim to be a basically good person will go to heaven, regardless of whether they've accepted Christ or even believe God exists. Why then, Benedict asks, should the Church even bother with evangelism? In answer, he turns the question around and asserts that it is un-Christian to see Christian service as worthwhile, only if others are condemned to eternal damnation. He joins the secular world in condemning as intolerant the biblical belief that hell awaits those who rebel against God. Evangelism is reduced to another service to the Church for the purposes of avoiding "spiritual unemployment," as he calls it, and to provide others with the option of following Christ as their path to heaven.[5]

The pope's influence, however, hasn't been limited to just religious movements and social issues. Many countries which have joined the United States in enforcing a separation of church and state make an exception when it comes to the Catholic Church, and routinely include them in policy discussions and international peace-keeping

---

5. Joseph Ratzinger, "Are Non-Christians Saved?" excerpted from "What It Means to Be a Christian," translated by Henry Taylor. Original German version published in 1965. Copyright 2006 by Ignatius Press, http://www.beliefnet.com/story /209/story_ 20936_1.html.

missions. The pope's opinion was widely reported, along with other world leaders, in the highly controversial negotiations prior to the Iraq War. The pope has even weighed in on the unification of Europe when, in the 1998 Feast of Ascension, he said, "Italy is called to contribute in its own way so that, in the new Europe, the Christian faith might be life-giving leaven and cement which unifies."

Many people, including Christians, would likely dismiss such a statement from the pope as nothing more than the opinion of one of the world's many religious leaders. However, they would be underestimating just how powerful Rome and the Vatican are in the world. Consider that the Vatican is the wealthiest organization on the planet! U.S. presidents and other dignitaries routinely visit the Vatican, and the pope frequently weighs in on Middle East policy and legislation relating to social issues in Europe and the United States, and often represents all of Christianity, whether protestant or Catholic, in organizations like the United Nations, and numerous global interfaith organizations.

While their global influence is important to our understanding of their role in prophecy, the Catholic Church is important to end-times prophecy for more than just their ecumenical views and contribution to the interfaith movement. Catholicism and the papacy can also be seen in the end-times Scriptures that prophecy a global religious system, which will come under the leadership of the False Prophet.

Wait a minute! Please do not hang up just yet. You may be thinking I am anti-Catholic and an enemy of anyone who is a Catholic. This is not true! I have many Catholic friends who are clearly born-again followers of Jesus Christ. That said, they themselves have told me they have come to understand "saving grace" in Christ alone in spite of the teachings of the church, not because of it! In addition, they have remained in the church and attempt to be salt and light to their friends.

Please do not put this book down. I urge you to understand just how the enemy, Satan, is at work through religion!

To understand Catholicism's future role, it is helpful to look briefly at the church's long history. Many Catholics are completely unaware that numerous heretical beliefs were introduced into Christianity through the Catholic Church. It's not a matter of intelligence in any way, but a simple matter of what members of the church are told by their leaders, coupled with a strong disapproval of self-study, or self-interpretation of the Bible from those same leaders. When speaking with Catholics, it's not uncommon to hear the claim made that the Catholic Church is the church founded by Jesus Himself, and is solely responsible for keeping the Christian faith alive through the centuries. They are well versed in an interpretation of Scripture that views Peter as the rock the church was founded upon, instead of Jesus, as the Bible teaches. Catholicism also maintains that Peter was the very first pope. In actuality, Peter was an Apostle to many peoples, in many places, but his time in Rome was limited to his imprisonment, and eventual crucifixion. If you make the argument that the papacy did not exist before the fifth century, you'll likely encounter a vigorous defense of a history that is vastly different from the version you'll find in the history books. It is this deception, and revisionist history that allows the Catholic Church to claim a higher authority than the Bible itself, and substitute church tradition for the Word of God.

While it is true that a large part of Christian history is found in the story of Catholicism's rise to power in the 4th century, followed by its supremacy during the Dark Ages, it's wholly untrue to say that it was, or is, based on the original teachings of Jesus. It was, in fact, responsible for taking the Word of God out of the hands of the people, and restricting its interpretation to church leaders, and ultimately the papacy. Under the dictates of reigning popes, Bibles were burned, chained to the pulpits of churches, banned from being printed and restricted from use by anyone but the clergy of the church. With church tradition elevated to a more accurate source for church doctrine, the Bible was seen as a threat to papal control over the masses. Allowed in the hands of laypersons, Scripture would shine a light of truth on the contradictions between the traditions of men, and the teachings of Christ and the Apostles. These traditions included things like indulgences for sins, and the belief that Christ must be re-sacrificed again and again in the form of the eucharist for the remission of future sins that are not covered by the blood of Christ. When these teachings came in conflict with the Word of God, the church needed to be able to correct "false interpretations" and promote a dependence on church leaders rather than Scripture.

This is not to say that Christians everywhere were deceived, and the Bible was lost to the ages. There have always been those who saw the truth of the Bible and listened to the counsel of the Holy Spirit. The cries of protest from these true believers led to the death of millions of Jews and Christians during the Spanish Inquisition, and birthed the Reformation under the leadership of Martin Luther as well as ultimately leading to the discovery of America.

Under the constantly changing traditions that were introduced at the whim of a succession of popes, Catholicism turned the Christianity of the Roman Empire into a works-based religion that elevates Mary to a status of co-redeemer (or co-matrix) with Jesus, and denies the saving power of Christ's sacrifice that was made ONCE FOR ALL. That sacrifice never needs to be helped along by confessions, sacraments, or the forgiveness of sins by mere men of leadership in the Catholic Church. Over the course of its history, and especially in today's atmosphere of ecumenism and tolerance, Catholicism did one other thing for the world. It created the perfect position of leadership, ideally suited for the False Prophet to use as a pulpit to present the Antichrist's global ambitions to the world, and establish, under his authority, a single global religion.

In fact, the leader of the Italian Democratic Party, Walter Veltroni, recently proposed the creation of an "Organization of Religions Nations" to be based in Rome, as a religious counterpart to the United Nations. Veltroni hopes to create a "Palace of

Religions" in Rome, similar to the United Nations building in the Turtle Bay neighborhood of midtown Manhattan. At this new palace in Rome, representatives from every religion in the world could come together to discuss the role of religion in the world. Rome's role in United Nations governance is well established, as it already headquarters to three United Nations agencies that deal with food and agriculture: International Fund for Agricultural Development, the Organization for Food and Agriculture, and Global Agenda Food.[6] Uniting the world's religions in Rome along with organizations dealing with the distribution of food fits perfectly into the end-times scenario that will see the False Prophet heading a global religious system, and controlling global commerce through a system of marking people.

The "United Religions," as Veltroni has called it, would take groups like the United Religions Initiative and the World Counsel of Churches to the next level, and create a central religious headquarters in the very city from which the Antichrist and False Prophet are to rise to power.

For the first half of the Tribulation, the Antichrist will benefit greatly from the vast resources, money, influence, and power that will be available to him through the cooperation of the Vatican and the pope, as well as this new United Religions headquarters backed by the United Nations. Using this pulpit, the False Prophet, who may very well end up being the pope himself, will bring before the world a new mystery religion displaying many miracles and signs that will unite the diverse religions of the planet around the Antichrist. However, this power will only be needed by the Antichrist for a time. Revelation 17, verses 16 and 17, states that at the midpoint of the Tribulation, the Beast will no longer need the woman and she will be destroyed. This will leave the Beast as the only source of unifying power, but with greater control over the population of the earth.

---

6. "One World Religion — Proposal to Create a Religious UN in Rome," http:// www.agi.it.

Then an angel said to me, "The waters you saw, where the prostitute sits are peoples, multitudes, nations and languages. The beast and the ten horns you saw will hate the prostitute. They will bring her to ruin and leave her naked; they will eat her flesh and burn her with fire. For God has put it into their hearts to accomplish His purpose by agreeing to give the beast their power to rule, until God's words are fulfilled. The woman you saw is the great city that rules over the kings of the earth (Revelation 17:15–18).

Why would the Antichrist and kings of the earth dismantle and cease to utilize the influence of this new religious system? He will do so, because half way through the Tribulation he will make himself the center of all religious beliefs, and officially declare himself to be the true God of the universe, and worthy of worship. With the world already united around one religion, the woman that rode into the Tribulation on the back of the Antichrist's global government will have served her purpose.

Before we look further into the papacy's role in the end times, and its connection to the False Prophet, I would like to take a closer look at the scriptural support for the Roman Catholic Church being at the heart of the world religion that will propel the Antichrist into power, and solidify his control over the globe.

Revelation 17 and 18 speak of a "woman" who is riding a scarlet beast, covered in blasphemous names, with 7 heads and 10 horns. These verses are a reference to the global religious system that will be used by the Antichrist to unite the world in a common cause. Will this religious leader intentionally deceive those left behind to endure the Tribulation? I do not think so. I personally believe this man will truly believe the Antichrist is God and that he is serving the Christ who has returned. Regrettably, he will be as deceived as those who he himself is deceiving.

In the first 15 verses of Revelation 17, John is invited by an angel carrying bowls of divine judgment to view religious Babylon or Babylon from a religious standpoint. When Babylon is mentioned in the Bible, it can be referring to the Babylonian religion, the city of Babylon, or the empire of Babylon. The use of a woman in describing Babylon here indicates that the angel is referring to the religious Babylon. We know this because, when a woman is used symbolically in Scripture, it is usually being used to convey a religious movement. Jehovah's wife or the Bride of Christ are used to symbolize a good religious system, while an evil woman, such as a prostitute, would represent an evil religion. For example, Matthew 13:33–35 tells the story of a woman who took leavened bread, a symbol of evil, and hid it in three measures of meal until it had worked through the entire dough. Another example is the teachings of the false prophetess Jezebel who sought to unite the church with the world, against God's command that His kingdom is not of this world (John 18:36).

In Revelation 17:5, this evil woman who rides in on the back of the beast is given the name "Mystery Babylon the great the mother of prostitutes and of the abominations of the earth," which is a title that covers all false religions that claim to be Christian in content. In the Old Testament, the word "abomination" always refers to the worship of idols. God called the religion that Nimrod founded centuries before Christ an "abomination." In fact, all of the Babylonian religions used idolatry. Therefore, when the woman in end-times Scripture is described as the mother of the abominations of the earth, we know that her mystery religious system will use idolatry as well. With Catholicism's use of rosaries, statues of Mary in worship ceremonies, and, of course, the pilgrimages by millions of Catholics yearly to worship at the sights of Marian apparitions, the Catholic Church is ideally suited to introduce a new system of idolatry to the world.

The woman in these verses is also described as a mystery that sits on a beast with seven heads, which are seven hills. It's no coincidence that Rome is a city which sits on seven hills, and has, for centuries, been the headquarters for the Vatican and the Roman Catholic Church.

We're given even further evidence that John was speaking of Rome in Revelation 17:10–11 when he says that, at the time of his writing, "Five [kings] have fallen, one is, the other is not yet come come." The five fallen kings he spoke of here were Egypt, Assyria, Babylon, Medo-Persia, and Greece. The city in power at the time that John wrote Revelation was Rome, and the king or empire that is still to come is the revived Roman Empire, or the European Union. The eighth king will be the Antichrist, who will rule over the European Union and the world during the Tribulation.

As I said, the papacy is in an ideal position of leadership, in the right city, at the right time to meet the needs of the False Prophet. The false religion of the end times will be a corrupted, worldly version of the real thing. How do we know this? We're told in Revelation 13 that the False Prophet will be disguised as a lamb, but he will speak like a dragon and deceive many. In other words, he will appear to be good, and even Christian, but he will be working for Satan.

The Catholic Church has been led for hundreds of years by apostates who change the grace of our God into a license for immorality and deny Jesus Christ our Sovereign and Lord. These men of history made themselves into the arbiters of salvation, the "Holy Fathers," and diminished Christ's sacrifice through traditions that demand certain works in exchange for the forgiveness of sins.

What other religion on earth, but Catholicism, claims their leader is infallible? Catholicism is the only form of Christianity in our society today that isn't roundly criticized and condemned as intolerant for teaching that their traditions and teachings are as infallible as the pope himself. Furthermore, if the pope can dictate what tradition is, then he can easily adopt the teachings of the Antichrist, and billions of people will be required to accept them as Scripture. There is no reason to question new teachings, after all, even if they contradict what the church taught previously. Catholicism has been evolving and changing with each new pope for centuries. Contradicting the Bible isn't a problem for most Catholics either, as the Word of God is not given the same infallible status among the vast majority of Catholics, or by those in leadership. When showing Catholics where their traditions don't agree with the original teachings of the Bible, it's not uncommon to hear them say that the Bible is merely a collection of fairy tales which have been corrupted over the centuries, and through numerous translations, making tradition necessary for retaining the Church's teachings over time.

It is this attitude of uncertainty about the accuracy of the Bible that makes unifying clearly contradictory religions possible. This move toward Christian unity has been underway for some time through programs like "Evangelism A.D. 2000," which brought together Christians and Protestants in an effort to evangelize around the world more effectively.

The Religion of the United Nations

Evangelism of a watered down, compromised version of the gospel is not only spreading through the Catholic Church, but through the work of interfaith organizations at the United Nations, often under the leadership of representatives from the Vatican. Most people would be surprised by just how religious the United Nations has actually become since its creation as a replacement for the League of Nations. Under programs like the "Ark of Hope"[7] (a pagan version of the ark of the covenant), the United Nations has taken part in the Vatican's goal of uniting the religions of the world as a means to achieving world peace, and eradicating religiously motivated conflicts and wars.

The U.N. has been anti-Christian in their mission and beliefs for a very long time, and they have found an ally in the Catholic Church because of their willingness to promote tolerance at the expense of truth. The United Nations Charter, the United Nations

---

7. Ben Rast, "Ark of Hope: The New Age Covenant," Contender Ministries, July 20, 2002, http://www.contenderministries.org/articles/arkofhope.php.

sponsored Earth Charter, and the Catholic Church all agree that religions should not claim to know the ONLY truth, and offer the ONLY path to salvation. This directly contradicts Jesus' own words when He said, "I am the way and the truth and the life. No one comes to the Father except through me" (John 14:6).

Pope John Paul himself said that one need not believe in Jesus Christ to be saved.[8] In the same way, the United Nations works through agreements like the United Religions Initiative (URI) to spread a new gospel based solely on tolerance, rather than a steadfast belief in any one deity, set of morals, or statement of beliefs.[9] Christians who forsake the literal teachings of the Bible for this new tolerant religion that is neither hot nor cold are playing right into Satan's hands, and preparing the way for the False Prophet's new Universal Church. God warned us in Revelation 3:15–17 about this lukewarm, end-times church.

> I know your deeds, that you are neither cold nor hot. I wish you were either one or the other. So, because you are lukewarm — neither hot nor cold — I am about to spit you out of my mouth. You say "I am rich; I have acquired wealth and do not need a thing." But you do not realize that you are wretched, pitiful, poor, blind, and naked.

Sadly, this describes perfectly a growing segment of the Christian churches in our world today, and no church has been more eager to adopt a new, more inclusive brand of Christianity than the Catholic Church. Pope Benedict continues his predecessor's policy of unity, regardless of what biblical doctrines must be compromised.

As Europe unites politically and economically, it will also need to unite its religious communities if it is to achieve the utopia and globalization of the planet that its leaders have been working toward since World War II.

---

8. Vatican Information Center, December 2000.
9. Ben Rast, "The URI: Bishop Swing's New World Religion," Contender Ministries, July 20, 2002, http://www.contenderministries.org/articles/uri.php.

The positions of authority that will be necessary to catapult the Antichrist and the False Prophet into power are being created now with the passage of the E.U. Constitutional Treaty, and the Catholic Church has the political clout, money, and influence to unite all religions under that same banner of peace and security. This will become even more necessary and inevitable during the desperate times that will follow the disappearance of every true Christian on the planet. In addition to the acceptance of the heretical Emergent Church movement, Black Liberation theology and its sister, Collective Salvation in America, is and will play a contributing role in the last days' religious system of the evil one. Wake up and pay attention! Every building with a cross is not necessarily a true church!

Chapter 7

THE TEMPLE REBUILT

The rebuilding of a Jewish Temple in Jerusalem may be the hottest single topic, politically speaking, in the world. I have stood numerous times on Mount Moriah in Jerusalem pondering when and how this feat will be accomplished. Recently, while teaching onsite in Jerusalem, I shared with my friends why this is such a hot potato topic. Rooted in Judaism is the belief that if they can rebuild the Temple, the Messiah will come and inhabit it while reigning over the earth. This belief drives the passionate desire to get the Temple built! On the other hand, the Muslim world believes the fable that it was from Mount Moriah that Mohammed ascended into the sky on his winged steed, El Baruck. Therefore, in 687 the Dome of the Rock project began. This massive shrine was completed in 691 over the "rock" from which Mohammed supposedly "took his flight" to Mecca, and is today considered one of the three holiest spots in Islam. These two conflicting thoughts are at the root of the conflict over the 35 acres known as the Temple Mount. Therefore, the rebuilding of a Temple on this site will be another of the future events that will shake the world. Let's delve deeper into this thought, and as Glenn Beck, former host of the wildly popular CNN show by the same name says, "This is what I know."

One of the darkest days in Jewish history occurred when, on September 8, A.D. 70, the Jewish Temple in Jerusalem was destroyed by the Roman General Titus. On that horrible day, more than one million Jews lost their lives. The Temple, a symbol of God's presence among the Jews, was no more. Some believe that the prophecies concerning the Jewish Temple were fulfilled before the Temple was destroyed in A.D. 70. However, in order to believe this, they have to ignore several end-times prophecies that have never been fulfilled in history, and must be fulfilled during the reign of the Antichrist.

Common Misinterpretation of Scripture

Before we look at the prophecies concerning the rebuilding of the Temple in the end times, I want to clear up one common misinterpretation of Scripture. There is a group of Christians called Amillennialists who believe that the prophecies concerning the rebuilding of the Temple have been fulfilled already, and the Temple's destruction was fulfilled in A.D. 70, when the Jewish Temple was destroyed by the Romans. Another similar view is that the end-times prophecies concerning the Temple were fulfilled in the Maccabean time of persecution, during the reign of Antiochus Epiphanies. While the events surrounding these time periods do seem to fulfill some of the Scriptures that foretell the defiling of the Temple and its utter destruction, one passage of Scripture from Daniel clearly indicates that the Temple mentioned in Daniel chapter 9 is a reference to a future Temple that will exist during the seven-year Tribulation and the reign of the Antichrist. Let's look at Daniel 9:26–27.

[26]After the sixty-two "sevens," the Anointed One will be cut off and will have nothing. The people of the ruler who will come will destroy the city and the sanctuary. The end will come like a flood: War will continue until the end, and desolations have been decreed. [27]He will confirm a covenant with many for one "seven." In the middle of the "seven" he will put an end to sacrifice and offering. And on a wing

of the temple he will set up an abomination that causes desolation, until the end that is decreed is poured out on him.

Amillennialists believe that the "He" at the beginning of verse 27 is referring to the Anointed One in verse 26, and is a reference to the Messiah's sacrifice on the Cross, and the new covenant that put an end to temple sacrifice. There are some problems with this interpretation, however. First, verse 27 states that "He will confirm a covenant with many for one 'seven.' " Obviously, the new covenant that Jesus established through His sacrifice on the Cross was not a seven-year covenant. It is an eternal covenant, lasting until Christ's return. The second problem is that Amillennialists interpret the pronoun "he" in verse 27 as referring to the "Anointed One" mentioned earlier in verse 26. The normal laws of reference are that the pronoun should refer back to the last preceding person mentioned, which would be the "ruler who will come" of verse 26, rather than the earlier reference to the Anointed One. This means that the ruler who will come, or the Antichrist, will make a covenant with the many (the Jews), and in the middle of the seven-year Tribulation he will put an end to Temple sacrifice and set up the abomination that causes desolation. This abomination, of course, is a reference to the image of the Beast that the False Prophet will erect on a wing of the Temple during the second half of the Tribulation (Revelation 13:14–15). Following Christ's sacrifice on the Cross, when He was "cut off," as it's put in verse 26, we're told that the people of the "ruler who will come" will destroy the Temple. We know that the Antichrist will come from Rome during the end times, so we can read into it that the Romans are the people who would destroy the Temple after Christ was cut off. That's exactly what happened in A.D. 70. After the Temple's destruction, these verses tell us that there would be a period of time when war would continue. This time gap between the first and second coming of Christ is confirmed by Old Testament Scripture, which allows for an inter-advent age interposed between references to the first and second coming of Christ.[1] We're told that this time period lasts until desolations have been decreed. In other words, it lasts until the Antichrist sets up the abomination that causes desolation in a wing of the Temple.

From all of this, we must conclude that a third Temple will be built, and the Jewish sacrificial system reestablished in order for the Antichrist to stop Temple sacrifice and offerings, and defile the Temple with his image. This is backed up by Daniel 12:11 which states that "from the time that the daily sacrifice is abolished and the abomination that causes desolation is set up, there will be 1,290 days," or three and a half years. Once again, the Temple sacrifice will be stopped halfway through the Tribulation, and three and a half years before Christ returns to defeat the Antichrist and establish His Millennial Kingdom.

How the Temple Might Be Built

You might be wondering how the Temple will be rebuilt on the Temple Mount when the Dome of the Rock currently stands exactly where the Jewish Temple must be rebuilt. It's a reasonable question, considering the Middle East conflict between the Palestinians and the Jews that has been raging for decades, despite efforts to resolve the conflict by every U.S. president and the world ever since the conflict began. There are several scenarios that would allow the Temple to be rebuilt, but we'll look at one possible scenario that seems most reasonable to me in light of current events and what the Scriptures tell us.

As we learned, the Rapture will be followed by a war in the Middle East that will leave the attacking Arab nations surrounding Israel completely decimated. In chapter 4, I theorized that it's entirely possible the Dome of the Rock may be taken out of the picture during the nuclear war and natural disasters God will use to supernaturally protect Israel from her attackers. Whether it's by destruction during war, or the result of an earthquake, we can be sure that the Dome of

---

1. John F. Walvoord, *Every Prophecy of the Bible* (Colorado Springs, CO: Chariot Victor Publishing, 1999), p. 256.

the Rock will be taken out of the way, to allow for a final end-times Jewish Temple to be built on the Temple Mount in the footprint of the previous two Temples.

The first three and a half years of the Tribulation will be relatively peaceful under the Antichrist's reign, and will give the remaining population of the planet a false sense of hope and security. While the rebuilding effort and recovery period after the Rapture will be slow, things will settle and return to a form of normalcy. The resiliency and strength we saw in the American people following 9/11, and in Europe following similar terrorist attacks, represents a common ability among human beings to face tragedy, unite with their fellow man, and return to their lives as quickly as possible. This eagerness we share to restore order and return to what is familiar will lead the world to unite following the Rapture, and do whatever it takes to restore peace, bring stability to a chaotic world, and guard against further devastation.

The Antichrist will seize upon people's desperate need to rebuild something better from the rubble left behind, and his mastery of diplomacy will be put to speedy use around the world. One of the most important peace-making endeavors that will be undertaken by the Antichrist in the beginning of the Tribulation period will be to finally restore peace to the Middle East. He will do what once seemed impossible, and negotiate a peace treaty between Israel, the Palestinians, and the Arab world, and as a part of that treaty, he will allow the Jews to rebuild their Temple on the Temple Mount.

In addition to the Antichrist's supernatural ability to win people to his position through diplomacy, it's possible that the Arab world will accept him as the returning 12th Imam of Islamic prophecy. Islamic leaders are already preparing for his return, and many leaders, including the president of Iran, have indicated that they believe the Mahdi's return is only a few years away. With the Arab world having suffered a devastating loss following their invasion of Israel, the Mahdi's return might represent at least a spiritual victory for the Islamic faith. Islamic prophecy teaches that the 12th Imam will return to extract revenge upon the unbelievers of the world, and especially the Jews.

How tempting it will be for a defeated people to place their hope in a man who may have arrived on the scene to snatch victory from the jaws of defeat and restore their honor. The Quran even teaches that a treaty may be negotiated with an enemy of Islam, if the resulting peace time can be used to rebuild your army and prepare for jihad.

We can also see a move toward the fulfillment of these prophecies in recent international efforts to divide Jerusalem and negotiate control of the Temple Mount. Revelation 11:1–3 gives us another clue as to how their negotiations may play out.

> I was given a reed like a measuring rod and was told "Go and measure the temple of God and the altar, and count the worshipers there. But exclude the outer court; do not measure it, because it has been given to the Gentiles. They will trample on the holy city for 42 months. And I will give power to my two witnesses, and they will prophecy for 1,260 days, clothed in sackcloth."

Before Israel was created as a Jewish nation, the 1947 General Assembly resolution that was to partition British Palestine into Jewish and Arab states called for Jerusalem to be internationalized — belonging to neither side.[2] This proposed solution to give sovereignty over the city to the nations was abandoned; however, when Israel captured East Jerusalem from Jordan in the 1967 Mideast War. Negotiations since 2000 have once again revived the idea of internationalizing the Holy City.

In September of 2000, the government of Israel promoted the idea of entrusting control of the Temple Mount to the United Nations, under the supervision of the five permanent members of the U.N. Security Council.[3] Then again in 2005, Shimon Peres, a former Israeli prime minister, proposed that Jerusalem be declared the "Capital of

---

2. "Jerusalem Touted as World's Capital," Worldnet Daily, 07/23/2003, http://www.worldnetdaily.com/news/article.asp ?ARTICLE_ID=33711.

3. Suzanne Goldenberg, "Israel Says UN Should Take Over Temple Mount," *The Guardian*, 09/25/2000, http://www.guardian. co.uk/world/2000/sep/25/israelandthepalestinians.united nations.

the World," putting all important religious shrines in Jerusalem under U.N. stewardship.

Today, world leaders have been pushing a proposal for Jerusalem that would divide the city, with East Jerusalem coming under Palestinian control, and giving total sovereignty over the Temple Mount to the Palestinians.

At the Annapolis Summit in 2007, George Bush and Israeli Prime Minister Olmert put Jerusalem on the altar of sacrifice once again in "The Final Status Plan," by calling for Israel to give up East Jerusalem for a future Palestinian state.[4]

It may be that Revelation 11:2 will be fulfilled as part of the Antichrist's peace agreement with Israel by dividing the Temple Mount and Jerusalem, and giving the Palestinians control of East Jerusalem, while requiring a court of the rebuilt Jewish Temple be used as a United Nations controlled "Capital of the World." Surrendering a court of their sacred Temple to the Gentiles would be a small sacrifice for Israel to make in order to gain sovereignty over the rest of the Temple Mount and rebuild their Temple.

Whether the city is divided or internationalized, the Antichrist will be able to convince the warring sides in the Middle East conflict to put aside their differences and begin the rebuilding of the Temple. A long-sought-after peace will appear to overtake the planet almost overnight. However, this peace will be a false peace; an illusion designed to hide the Antichrist's true plans for the planet, which are being worked out behind the scenes.

Exactly 1,290 days, or 3½ years after the Tribulation begins, the peace he negotiated and restored around the world will disintegrate. The second half of the Tribulation will begin the Great Tribulation. This time of punishment and wrath on earth will be kicked off by the Antichrist breaking the covenant he made with Israel, and bringing an end to the Jewish system of sacrifice for the atonement

4. Aaron Klein, "Jerusalem to be Divided, Declares Israeli Official," Worldnet Daily, 12/09/2007, http://www.worldnetdaily.com/news/article.asp?ARTICLE_ID=59119.

of sins. Even more insulting to the Jewish people, the Antichrist will erect an image of himself in a wing of the Temple. This is the image of the Beast that everyone will be required to worship in order to receive their mark of loyalty. It's likely that this image will use some kind of holographic technology to make the Antichrist appear to be in two places at once. Scientists have already developed a technique for displaying three-dimensional holographic images, an innovation that they hope will soon enable doctors to perform virtual surgeries, and produce 3D medical imaging studies instead of the two-dimensional MRIs and CAT scans currently in use. They also predict it will be useful in military field simulations, and in things like advertising billboards.[5] This technology would be ideal for bringing the antichrist's image to life in a wing of the Temple.

After three and a half years of peace, and a very convincing display of signs, wonders, and miracles around the world, the Antichrist will finally take the title many people will have already assigned to him. He will declare to the world that he is the God of the universe. Having suffered a fatal wound and come back to life, he will claim to be the returned Christ, the Imam Mahdi, and the fulfillment of every religion on earth's final destiny. Every person alive will be required, under penalty of death, to worship the Antichrist, or at the very least, bow before the image of their new god that will be set up in the Jewish Temple.

Jewish Views on Temple Restoration

We've established that the Antichrist will have a purpose for seeing the rebuilding of the Temple in Jerusalem, but how do the Jews in Israel feel about the restoration of their sacred Temple? For the Jewish people, rebuilding their Temple has been a dream since its destruction nearly 2,000 years ago. Longing for the Temple to be rebuilt is so much a part of the life of religious Jews in Israel that Orthodox Jews pray for its restoration three times a day. It's even a

---

5. "Breakthrough Helps 3D Holograms Come to Life," CBC News, 2/6/2008, http://www.cbc.ca/technology/story/2008/02/06 /techholographmoveable.html.

part of Jewish wedding ceremonies. During the marriage ceremony a goblet is broken, symbolizing the couple's solidarity with other Jews in mourning the loss of their Temple. A day of mourning is also observed annually on the anniversary of the Temple's destruction, on the 9th of Av. Both the first and second Temples were destroyed on this same day in history. The first Temple was destroyed by the Babylonians in 586 B.C., 364 years after it was built. Then in A.D. 70, just 6 years after the enlargement and beautification of the Temple begun during the reign of Herod the Great was completed, the Roman 10th Legion sacked Jerusalem, destroyed the Temple, and took with them many of the sacred vessels and religious artifacts from within.

It has been the Jews' goal to rebuild once again on the Temple Mount since A.D. 70. Their dream of a third Temple seemed within their grasp when Israel became a nation again in 1948. One Jewish group in particular has been leading an effort to prepare for the rebuilding of the Temple. The Temple Mount Faithful, as the movement's followers are called, led by Rabbi Chaim Richmond and Gershon Salomon of the Temple Institute, not only want to rebuild a Temple where the previous two Temples stood, but they hope to reinstitute the sacrificial system of the Old Testament. The Temple Mount and Eretz Yisrael (Land of Israel) Faithful Movement was founded by former Israeli Defense Forces officer and Middle Eastern Studies lecturer Gershon Salomon with the goal of preparing for the day that the Jews in Israel will rebuild their Temple, and resume ritual sacrifices for the atonement of their sins. In preparation for the day when their beloved Temple is rebuilt, they have been recreating the ancient Temple vessels necessary for proper worship in the Temple and training rabbis for worship ceremonies in accordance with Old Testament law.

I've had the opportunity on several occasions to speak with Rabbi Richmond. One meeting sticks out in my mind. He said of the Temple, "The Shekinah is brought about only through the Temple. In terms of our mission as a people, we cannot in any way reach our spiritual status without the Temple." It is for this reason that the Temple Mount Faithful work so diligently to heighten awareness and understanding of the Temple's importance among both Jews and Christians, as they go about the business of preparing the religious articles that will be needed for proper worship in a third Temple.

Gershon Solomon believes that the Temple will be rebuilt very soon, and he wants to renew everything that belongs to the Temple and biblical tradition. In an attempt to restore some of the original sacred vessels from the first and second Temples, the Temple Mount Faithful have even written to the Pope himself. In the letter, Rabbi Salomon wrote the following words to the Roman Catholic Church:

> As you well know, in 70 CE the Romans occupied the City of G-d, Yerushalaim, and the Land of Israel and destroyed the Holy Temple of the Gd of Israel in Yerushalaim. They took away with them to Rome the holy Seven-Branch Menorah from the Temple and many other holy Temple vessels and treasures used by the Jews in the worship in the Temple. The evil emperor, Titus, who destroyed the Temple and burned it, built his Triumphal Arch in Rome on which is depicted the Menorah and other vessels carried by Jewish captives. Since this terrible event in the history of Israel and mankind, we know very well that the Menorah, the vessels and the treasures that were taken to Rome have remained in the vaults of the Vatican. Travelers and visitors to the Vatican throughout history have reported seeing them.[6]

He went on to demand that the Temple Menorah, vessels, and Temple treasures be immediately returned to Jerusalem, and to the soon-to-be-rebuilt Temple.

The Bible says that the daily sacrifice will be re-established during the first half of the Tribulation. This means that the Temple

---

6. "The Temple Mount Faithful Movement Letter to the Pope," B'ezrat HaShem, 01/22/2004, http://www.templemountfaithful.org/News/20040209.htm.

must be rebuilt on the Temple Mount. The third Temple won't just be the dream of religious Jews in Israel. The Antichrist himself will want and need the Temple rebuilt. Groups like the Temple Mount Faithful are, unbeknownst to them, preparing the Temple vessels and articles for the Antichrist to use when he makes, and then breaks, a covenant with Israel, and defiles the Temple with an image of himself in place of the true God of the Bible. Only a literal, physical, stone and mortar Temple built on the Temple Mount could fulfill this end-times prophecy. Where the Western Wall now stands, and the shimmering, gold Dome of the Rock dominates the Jerusalem skyline, a Jewish Temple will be rebuilt in all its glory, and the Jewish people will celebrate the return of the Shekinah Glory to the Holy City of Jerusalem. But this celebration will only last for a short time.

Chapter 8

THE MARK

Several years ago while visiting London I walked through my hotel lobby and out onto the street looking for a newspaper vending machine. At the corner, I found not one but two machines. I looked at the machines, and noticed one was a standard coin vending machine. The second machine, however, took only smart cards. I stood there for a moment and recalled an article I had read a few months before. This particular article appeared in *P.C. Computing* magazine, and was written by Paul Somerson. The entire article was about the emerging new technology of biochip implants and how they would be marketed to the masses. The final paragraph was so compelling I have never forgotten it. Somerson said, "How will they convince people to implant these chips? First, they'll hype the convenience of leaving your keys, credit cards, and money at home. Then they'll automate everything from cash registers to tollbooths, so if you're chipped, you can zoom through in a digital carpool lane."[1] I realized the transition from cash to implant technology would happen gradually and that our society would hardly be

---

1. Paul Somerson, "Would Life Be Better?" PC Computing ZDNN, September 27, 1999, http://www.bibliotecapleyades.net/ciencia/secret_projects/project181.htm.

cognizant it was even taking place. Today the pace has quickened and one need only look at the world around them to see that it is everywhere. We have been given the pitch, and we have bought into this convenient tool, hook, line, and sinker!

Before we look at how this technology will fulfill end-times prophecy, let's review where we are in our study of God's prophetic time-line. The first three and a half years of the Tribulation will see plagues visited on the people of the earth, a meteorite will poison the waters, warring enemies will kill millions, those who take the mark of the Beast will be tormented by demonic locusts, and half of the world's post-Rapture population will die. And it gets worse. The last three and a half years of the Tribulation are referred to in scripture as the Great Tribulation, and for good reason. Matthew 24:21–22 says, "For then there will be great distress, unequaled from the beginning of the world until now — and never to be equaled again. If those days had not been cut short, no one would survive, but for the sake of the elect those days will be shortened." God is patient with us, because He loves us and wants everyone to come to a saving relationship with Him, but during the final three and a half years of the Tribulation, God's patience with a sinful, rebellious world will come to an end, and His wrath will finally be poured out on those who chose to follow the Antichrist and worship him as God (Revelation 15:78).

Revelation 13, 17, and 18 describe what a world under the Antichrist's rule will look like during the Great Tribulation. During this time, the Antichrist and the False Prophet will have total control of the world's economy, and all commerce on a global scale, as well as at the local level. The False Prophet will be able to exercise this control, under the Antichrist's authority, by using what Scripture calls the "mark of the beast." Revelation 13:15–17 says of the False Prophet, "He was given power to give breath to the image of the first beast, so that it could speak and cause all who refused to worship the image to be killed. He also forced everyone, small and great, rich and poor, free and slave, to receive a mark on his right hand or on his forehead, so that no one could buy or sell unless he had the mark, which is the name of the beast or the number of his name." The False Prophet will establish a global system of commerce that requires every person on earth to have the mark of the beast before they can buy or sell anything, and in order to get that mark one must worship the Antichrist and accept him as Lord. If anyone refuses to worship the beast and take his mark, they will face death. This means those Christians who accept Christ after the Rapture will be forced to make a very difficult choice. Those who choose to worship the Antichrist may escape an early physical death. However, they will pay with their eternal soul. Revelation 14:9–11 says that those who worship the beast, or the image of the beast, are, in effect, selling their souls to the devil. Burning sulfur and the smoke of their torment will rise for eternity, and there will be no rest for them.

The True Purpose of the Mark

The purpose of the mark is not necessarily to regulate who may buy and sell, although that's a part of it, but to force people to worship the Antichrist. By making the cost of refusing to do so as painful as possible, the Antichrist seeks to gain the worship and devotion of as many people as possible in the short time that he's in power. People often ask me what will happen to a person who takes the mark accidentally, or who is forced to take the mark against their will. I would like to reassure all of you that no Christian need fear taking the mark of the beast without their consent or knowledge. If a person has accepted Christ as their Savior following the Rapture, they can't accidentally take the mark, or receive it against their will. Followers of Christ already have a mark, and they are sealed by the blood of Christ. The mark of the beast is also a choice, and even the Antichrist presents it this way, albeit a choice with a very persuasive consequence for not complying with the Antichrist's desire to be worshiped by man. I assure you, God will give us the strength to face death for our faith if that's the choice we must make. If you think about it, this also makes sense from the perspective of what Scripture tells us about the Antichrist's motives for using a mark of loyalty. Indwelt by Satan, the Antichrist will eagerly seek to kill the followers of his most despised enemy, and stamp out the spread of the gospel during the Tribulation. It's not in his interests to force the mark on those who are loyal to the God of the Bible, and leave them alive to reach even one more soul for Christ.

In Revelation 13:16 and 17, we learn that the mark will be given on the right hand or on the forehead of those who choose to receive it, and it will somehow incorporate the name of the beast, or the number of his name. This number is man's number, or six hundred and sixty six (not six, six, six as it is commonly, but erroneously interpreted). The Antichrist and False Prophet will likely incorporate some form of technology into the administration of the mark in order to track and identify those who are, or are not, loyal to the Antichrist. However, that technology, in whatever form, will not constitute the mark of the beast. The Book of Revelation repeats eight times that the mark will include the Antichrist's number, and in Revelation 13 the Greek word *karigma* is used, which means, "to engrave upon." A visible mark will be engraved into the flesh of each of the Antichrist's devotees in the form of a tattoo. Tattoos have long been a popular form of body art among young people, members of the military, gang members, bikers, and the like. In fact, this form of body art has been popular among groups of people from every socioeconomic background throughout history, and it no longer carries the stigma that it once did in our culture. Most people today wouldn't think twice about getting a tattoo in order to express support for something they truly believe in.

The Tech Talk behind the Mark

At a recent Greener Gadgets Design Competition, engineer Jim Mielke introduced a wireless blood-fueled display that will merge cell phone technology with body art. He demonstrated a subcutaneously implanted touch screen that operates as a cell phone display, visible just underneath the skin. The display looks much like a tattoo, but the digital display is actually a Bluetooth compatible device made of silicon and silicone. It's inserted under the skin through a small incision, and then the tightly rolled tube unfurls between the muscle and skin. Two small tubes inserted with the device are attached to an artery and a vein, allowing blood to flow to a coin-sized blood fuel cell that converts glucose and oxygen in the blood into electricity. Instead of ink, the display uses tiny microscopic spheres, similar to tattoo ink, that create a touch screen on the skin. The tattoo display communicates wirelessly around the world, and in the same body, in much the same way that Bluetooth-compatible smart phones communicate with printers, cell phones, fax machines, and other Bluetooth-equipped devices. By pushing a small dot on the skin, the tattoo comes to life as a digital video of another caller, or any image that can be accessed wirelessly.

The new device isn't just useful in wireless communications. It also offers health benefits, as it continually monitors the implanted person for many blood disorders, alerting the person of any health problems it detects. With benefits like that, this new technology would be an easy sell in a technology-hungry world that is already dependent on smart phones, computers, and wireless internet. The tattoo display is still a concept in the development phase, but there is certainly a market for it among the millions of blackberry and iphone users around the world. Combined with GPS technology and electronic payment systems, these digital tattoos would be ideal for the Antichrist's system of marking those who are loyal to him.[2]

If, as you read the previous paragraphs, you were trying to cover up that tattoo on your arm, you don't need to. Having a tattoo doesn't mean you aren't a believer, and you haven't taken the mark of the beast. The mark doesn't come into play until the second half of the Tribulation and the Antichrist's ultimate purpose in imposing this system isn't to mark those who are loyal to him, or even to

2. "Preparing the Way for the Mark — Introducing Digital Tattoo Interface," http://www.physorg.com/news122819670.html.

control the world's economy, although those factors will aid in achieving his ultimate goal. His purpose is to fulfill his desire to be worshiped by man. Everyone will be required to take the mark under penalty of death, but in order to receive the mark people will be required to worship the Antichrist as Lord. It is this worship, and not the mark itself, that seals ones fate, and dooms a person's soul to eternal torment in hell. This is why believers need not worry that they will "accidentally" take the mark of the beast. No true believer would ever worship the Antichrist, or any other god for that matter. Since this is a requirement for receiving the mark, believers during the second half of the Tribulation will never find themselves in a situation where they've accidentally accepted a tattoo that they later find out is the mark of the beast.

The False Prophet will not be able to strictly enforce laws prohibiting Christians and other dissidents from buying and selling goods by use of a tattoo alone, which is key to persuading millions to accept the mark and worship the Antichrist. A global system that gives the Antichrist total control of the world's economy will be needed to enforce such strict laws regarding the worship of the Antichrist and the administration of the mark.

For centuries the idea that one man could control the world's economy and restrict commerce on a global, national, and local level, seemed like the stuff of science fiction. However, today's rapid technological advances, and the rise of the computer age has changed that. You might be surprised to learn that the technology for implementing just such a system of marking people and regulating their ability to buy or sell already exists, and is in use in various forms around the world. The last decade has seen a steady march toward the global, technology-driven, government-controlled and regulated economy that will allow one man to control everything.

Getting Rid of Old Fashioned Cash

This shift toward globalization can be seen in the economies of many countries, their health care systems, and in free trade agreements around the world. The change most important to the Antichrist's future enforcement of the mark is a shift toward a cashless society. It wasn't just convenience that led society to begin replacing coins and paper currency with checkbooks, debit cards, and credit cards. Likewise, smart cards, electronic purses, and contactless payment systems aren't just the latest marketing scheme created to attract new customers. They are a calculated move toward a cashless society, and this shift is happening on a global scale.

There are many benefits to eliminating the use of cash for governments, businesses, and consumers alike. A cashless global economy would help in crime prevention, fraud, and the sale of weapons, just to name a few. However, there is a very big down side to a high-tech, cashless society. Ending the use of cash takes power away from regular people, and puts it in the hands of governments and world leaders. In other words, he who controls the money has all the power. With cash in your pocket you can buy, sell, travel, trade, and live without any government involvement in your life. Without cash, you become dependent on some other entity for your entire existence, and much of what you do, and where you go becomes public information. This is why it's only in a cashless society that the Antichrist will be able to control who is allowed to buy and sell.

Technological advances already in use today will allow the Antichrist to track and monitor every person on the planet. As we'll see, advances in the area of commerce, banking, medical care, and government services are already coming together on a regional basis and the plan is, and has always been, to integrate these systems into a cashless global economy. The elimination of cash as our system of payment has been the goal for decades, but it is only now that the means to do so are available to the governments, world leaders, and bankers who negotiate trade agreements and make our global economy work.

The process begins with the regionalization of the planet; the most obvious example being the formation of the European Union. This isn't the only region, however, where a regional economy is uniting countries and replacing nationalism with regional cooperation and integration. In the southern hemisphere, the African continent is working toward an African Union, and South American countries are working together toward a future South American Union. Even the United States is steadily working toward an end to national sovereignty, and the creation of a North American Union. Though very little is ever mentioned about it in the media, Congress is actively working and voting on legislation that will lead to one regional North American currency, one continental transportation system, integrated labor mobility, and the integration of security and defense for the continent. Daniel Estulin, the author of two best-selling books, *The True Story of the Bilderberger Group* and *The Late Great USA*, which documents the move toward an American Union, is quoted as saying, "Everything is in place. Europe is now one country, one currency, and one constitution. North America is about to become one. The African Union has had its working model going for over a decade. Asia is openly discussing the near future Asian Union, being sold to us as an economic inevitability beneficial to all citizens."[3]

In the United States, the controversial immigration reform bill of 2007 contained provisions for the acceleration of the "Security and Prosperity Partnership" (SPP), a plan for North American economic and defense integration that is strikingly similar to the early stages of the European Union. The SPP agreement was signed by President Bush and his counterparts in Mexico and Canada in 2005, and has since been labeled by critics as a blueprint for a European style American Union. This rush toward creating regions of economic and defense cooperation will be the key to the fulfillment of the prophesied ten regions in the Antichrists global government, as represented by the ten toes and ten horns in Daniel's dreams. It will also be an integral step toward a global system of commerce, and the

---

3. "North American Union a Couple of years Away," 11/29/2007, http://worldnetdaily.comY

mark of the beast. Negotiations, treaties, and agreements are already being discussed and legislated to merge these regional unions into a high tech, cashless global system.[4]

So why is the world in such a rush to get rid of cash in favor of technology-dependent trade and commerce? There are many reasons, and most of them are not new. The primary reason for doing away with national currencies is the enormous losses banks, governments, and businesses incur every year due to fraud, counterfeiting, crime, and lost tax revenue from under the table cash transactions.

World leaders are correct in theorizing that many of the world's problems will go away, or be greatly improved, when cash has been fazed out and replaced. The elimination of cash will benefit every person on the planet, but those in power stand to gain the most from a new system.

Billions of dollars in taxes go unpaid every year when people make sales and purchases under the table using cash. If a cashless system were the only means for making these transactions, governments would be able to collect sales tax on everything that is bought or sold, including sales made between family members, or even the purchase of something at a garage sale.

In addition to the loss of tax revenue from cash transactions, governments and financial institutions lose billions to fraud each year. Without cash, crimes such as money laundering, bank fraud, and the corporate scandals that broke during President Bush's first term in office would be nearly impossible.

Increased government revenue isn't the only monetary benefit countries will see with the elimination of cash. A cashless system would have a huge impact on crime around the world. Counterfeiting would cease, saving banks, businesses, and governments billions of dollars. Without cash, drug trafficking would be greatly reduced and would become a far less lucrative business overnight. The sale of guns would be far easier for governments to track, monitor, and

---

4. "North American Union Plan Headed to Congress in Fall," 05/24/2007, http://worldnetdaily.com.

put restrictions on, and gun laws would be easier to enforce. With illegal guns, and guns obtained for the purposes of committing crimes only available in trade or by stealing them, violent crimes involving guns would likely plummet, as would gun ownership among law-abiding citizens. U.S. politicians would finally be able to regulate and monitor gun shows and gun ownership by law-abiding citizens, bringing them that much closer to taking away our Second Amendment right to keep and bear arms.

A selling point for a government-controlled system of commerce that would be especially popular in today's political climate is the effect it would have on illegal immigration. Illegal aliens crossing the border from Mexico or abroad would no longer be able to escape detection from INS. Cash payments for the millions of jobs now filled by illegal migrant workers would end, making it impossible to live in the United States without citizenship. Every necessity of life, including medication, food, housing, and medical care would require a method of payment that doesn't allow for anonymity. Making it more difficult to live in the United States illegally would also make it harder for many of the terrorist cells that currently operate undetected to plot their attacks. Muhammad Atta and his band of terrorists might not have been able to successfully execute the attacks of September 11 if every transaction made within the country were traceable by our intelligence agencies. The funding schemes set up by Islamic front groups and phony charities could never operate openly as they did prior to 9/11 in a cashless society.

Before a global economy can be controlled, government control of commerce must be established on a smaller scale within nations, and then regions. As I stated earlier, the United States, Canada, and Mexico have been working toward a North American Union, with plans for a regional currency called the amero. These regional currencies will lay the groundwork for a future global currency.

Most people are completely unaware that the United States Congress has been working on legislation for the creation of a North American Union, or NAU, as well as a regional currency called the amero, for some time. Congress submitted a final report to the White House in the summer of 2007, detailing the benefits of integrating the United States, Mexico, and Canada into one political, economic, and security bloc. The approved report is to be submitted to all three governments as a guideline for policymakers to begin legislating regional integration. Under the new guidelines, the three countries will address labor mobility, energy, the environment, security, and the unification of economies, including a single North American currency.[5]

The Immigration Reform Act of 2007 also included provisions for the acceleration of the SPP, a plan for North American integration on economic and defense level that will begin the process of legislating the report. This legislation was met with a firestorm of opposition and complaints that the bill amounted to nothing less than an amnesty program. However, it's only a matter of time before economic woes, out of control illegal immigration, and the terrorist threat will sway the American public. This is especially true of a looming economic crisis that will result from the fall of the U.S. dollar as the reserve currency of the world.[6]

The Fall of the U.S. Dollar

As was discussed in chapter 4, Iran is replacing the dollar as the currency used for the sale of oil around the world. This aggressive move by Iran may not be necessary, however, since the value of the dollar is already declining rapidly. The dollar is currently losing its status as the world currency as a result of globalization and a stronger euro. In the closing days of 2007, a sharp drop in the dollar against other major currencies brought the greenback to a record low of $1.50 to the euro in New York trading. This was the lowest level in 57 years against the Canadian dollar, the British pound, and other currencies.[7] The fast rate of depreciation of the U.S. dollar is fueling

---

5. Ibid.
6. Ibid.
7. "China Signals Dollar Swap, Dow Plunges," 11/8/2007, *Washington Times*, http://washingtontimes.com.

fears that it will scare away investment by foreign countries. China, with the largest reserve of U.S. dollars, has already begun divesting its Treasury holdings and is now diversifying its investments by purchasing stock in other countries and moving its reserve dollars to euros. Other European countries, including France and Britain, have threatened economic retaliation if the United States does not take responsibility for their debt, get their financial house in order, and promote fair exchange rates.[8]

The falling dollar is serious business and, if it's not dealt with properly, it could lead to an economic collapse that would make a regional or even world currency look much more appealing to the majority of Americans. The SPP working groups, as well as the Council on Foreign Relations, are well aware of this dilemma, and have been working on the creation of the "amero" as a solution for some time. The plan is to create an E.U. style currency and have a North American Central Bank sit over the Bank of Canada and the Federal Reserve Bank in the United States.[9]

The Federal Reserve currently faces a situation that poses dire consequences for all of us. If the Fed raises interest rates to prop up the dollar, we could fall into a recession. On the other hand, if they lower interest rates further to stimulate the economy it would erode the dollar and spark massive inflation. Several prominent investors have voiced concerns that America may be sitting on a collapse that could make the economic conditions of 1979 and 1980 look rosy by comparison.[10]

America has been spending more money than it brings in for a very long time. The only thing that keeps America afloat is its ability to borrow money from other countries, and those countries are growing weary of loaning us money, only to have our currency

8. Peter S.Goodman, "China Set to Reduce Exposure to Dollar," *Washington Post*, 1/10/2006, http://washingtonpost.com.
9. Jerome Corsi, "Billionaire to Canada: Time for Amero Is Now," Worldnet Daily, 11/27/2007, http://wnd.com/news/article.asp? ARTICLE_ID=5887.
10. "Alarm: China Signals Flight from Dollar," WorldNetDaily, 11/7/2007, http://www.wnd.com/news/article.asp? ARTICLE_ID=58563.

continue to lose its value. The only answer aside from following the E.U. model of unification is to live within our means, something politicians are good at promising during campaign season, but never live up to once they've been elected.

America's leaders have long known that globalization and free trade would lead to greater dependence on foreign economies and a need to integrate with those economies if we are to remain competitive in the world and maintain our national wealth. The creation of the European Union served to hasten a commitment from Europe and the United States to work toward deeper transatlantic economic integration. Toward that end, President Bush signed an agreement in 2007 that commits the United States to economic integration with Europe, and acknowledges that "the transatlantic economy remains at the forefront of globalization."[11]

In the agreement, the Transatlantic Economic Council (TEC) was tasked with creating regulatory convergence between the United States and the E.U., including integrating health industries, international trade, Generally Accepted Accounting Principles (GAAP), and implementing RFID (Radio Frequency Identifier) technologies. It is this cooperation on the implementation of RFID technologies that is of particular interest to us as we study what Scripture says about a global system of marking those who are loyal to the Antichrist. The TEC is working toward the same kind of integration and merger of policies that America has been working on with Mexico and Canada in the Security and Prosperity Partnership of North America, and it is in this regional merger that we can see the technology for the mark of the beast already being used.

The integration of technology and regulatory systems is at the heart of regional and global cooperation, and will be an absolute necessity if regional currencies, national security systems, healthcare, and governments are to be integrated into a North American Union and, eventually, a global system. RFID is the next logical step toward

11. Jerome Corsi, "Bush OK's 'Integration' with European Union," Worldnet Daily, 5/08/2007, http://www.worldnetdaily.com.

controlling commerce and regionalizing governments, and it also has great potential as a tool for tracking and monitoring commerce in the Antichrist's global government.

So, What Is Radio Frequency Identification?

RFID is a technology that uses a transponder tag to store information, which is later accessed and retrieved by an antenna that transmits a signal from the tag. Chipless RFID allows the tag to be imprinted directly in assets, where they can then be tracked and monitored throughout the supply chain. RFID has already been used in merchandise tracking in the United States and Europe, as well as in transportation systems, passports, product tracking, in automobiles, for animal identification as an implantable chip, and in inventory systems, libraries, schools, and universities. It has even been used in humans, such as Alzheimer patients, who can become easily lost and unable to identify themselves to others.

As RFID technology is being integrated into national and regional economies, agreements are also being made to ensure the inter-operability of these systems on a global level. In an April 30, 2007, White House press release, the Bush Administration made public a framework for advancing transatlantic integration. The framework was the result of an E.U.-U.S. Summit, chaired by a cabinet level official for the United States and a member of the European Commission, collaborating closely with the E.U. presidency on the E.U. side. In Annex 2, titled "Lighthouse Priority Projects," section D on innovation and technology states the following: "We resolve to: Develop a joint framework of cooperation on identification and development of best practices for radiofrequency identification (RFID) technologies and develop a work plan to promote the interoperability of electronic health record systems."

Annex 7 titled "Innovation and Technology" further states that the "U.S. and E.U. resolve to work together on interoperability of ehealth records systems, exchange best practices on all dimensions related to all RFID, and develop a framework of regulation and payment policies that promote innovation." All parties agreed to collaborate on innovation indicators and how data helps policymakers understand what drives innovation and its effects on economic performance.[12]

In short, the TEC and the United States agreed to work together to integrate their healthcare and economic systems with RFID technology that can later be merged into one system.

Most Americans aren't aware of just how successful the United States and Europe have been in the last decade at integrating RFID into our society. Passports were recently equipped with RFID tags that can be scanned at access points around the globe. With the War on Terror and border security on everyone's mind, we have stopped seeing this kind of data collection and tracking systems as an invasion of our privacy and the process of desensitizing us to these abuses of power is sure to continue.

Across the United States, subway systems, toll booths, and other forms of transportation are increasingly moving toward a contactless method of payment for commuters and those who use public transportation. For example, in Tacoma, Washington, the new Narrows Bridge was equipped with RFID readers that allow commuters to pay their toll in advance, eliminating the traffic clogging process of paying a toll each time you cross the bridge. The "Good to Go" toll system, as it's called, allows drivers to cross the Puget Sound without stopping at a toll booth. It does so by linking a prepaid account with an RFID transponder that is installed on the driver's vehicle. Each time the RFID-equipped vehicle crosses the eastbound side of the bridge a series of cameras snap 24 photographs, and a record of the date and time is stored in a database along with information identifying the persons "Good to Go" account. A computer then checks the image to verify that there

---

12. "Framework for Advancing Transatlantic Economic Integration between the United States of America and the European Union," Office of the Press Secretary, 4/30/2007, http://www.Whitehouse.gov.

is enough money in the corresponding account. Each commuter using the system leaves behind a record of their travels that will be open to criminal investigators and by court order for 8½ years. The stored data and images can also be used in civil cases, by employers involved in a lawsuit with an employee, or in divorce and custody battles.[13]

San Francisco uses a similar program on eight of its bridges, and new systems are being implemented in cities, large and small, across the country every year. As people use subways, buses, enter universities, libraries, government buildings, and corporate offices, they are leaving a record of their day. This ability to track the movement of individuals in a society seems harmless and quite convenient when it is examined as part of a local government system, but imagine how this kind of technology could be abused by regional and global government agencies. RFID by itself is dangerous enough, but transponders passing through checkpoints and recording a few moments of your life are only one piece of the technological puzzle that world leaders are putting together. When you combine RFID technology with Smart Cards, biometric national ID cards, and implantable chip technology, the picture darkens and the mark of the beast becomes a real possibility in our very near future.

Smart Cards

National identification cards with "smart card" technology will play a large part in a future global system. A global government could never be brought together from the merger of differing national systems, each with their own technology, methods of tracking and verifying citizenship, and forms of identification. Reliable, tamperproof, and accurate identification on a national level is the first necessary step, but the regionalization of citizenship identification in a way that is interoperable with other regions will

---

13. "New Narrows Bridge Finally Opens," Komo TV, 7/15/2007, http://komotv.com.

ultimately be required for the global control of commerce. This, too, is already being legislated in Europe, the United States, Mexico, South America, and other nations.

Europe has already developed and is using technology that incorporates RFID tags into the fibers of banknotes, allowing the government, banks, and businesses to track the history of transactions in every single banknote.[14] A new version of the UPC codes on products are also being replaced with Electronic Production Codes (EPCs) in stores like Walmart, Philip Morris USA, and Pfizer. EPCs use RFID to send and receive data information, allowing manufacturers to track and monitor their entire inventory. This technology will allow a police officer to determine the contents of your car by simply scanning the trunk with an RFID reader for the signal from EPCs embedded at the time of production.[15] The next logical step is to have the already existent RFID-equipped systems in vending machines and toll booths equipped with contactless payment systems. This will allow customers to pass through a reader and have their accounts automatically debited for their purchases.

Passports have been equipped with RFID tags that contain a small database of personal information, accessible to anyone with a reader, since August 2006. This same technology will likely be used in the national ID cards being proposed in Europe and the United States.

Former Prime Minister Tony Blair put a great deal of effort into promoting the need for a biometric national ID card for Britain, and eventually the European Union. In an e-mail to his critics posted on his website, Blair said that it would be foolish not to take the opportunity to use biometric data like fingerprints to secure a person's identity. He wrote that terrorists routinely use false identification to plot terrorist attacks and live among those they intend to kill. He also pointed out the need for ID cards in

---

14. Jake Perron, "Life Keeps Getting Easier and Scarier," *MinnesotaDaily*,
    10/08/2007, http://www.mndaily.com/articles /2007/10 /05/52163709.
15. Ibid.

order to combat illegal immigration, most notably the growing illegal immigration of Arabs from Muslim countries, and to fight forgery, fraud, and crime. His efforts were successful and, under Blair's leadership, legislation passed that will make a national ID card required by every British citizen by 2008–09. Ultimately the new administration repealed this but it is only a matter of time until this will be seen as a necessity for security. Such identification hasn't been required in Britain since World War II.[16]

Also in effect is an E.U. health ID card similar to the Smart Cards already used in Mexico and countries in South America. This new E.U.-wide health system will store biometric and personal data on a microchip that will be embedded in an ID card.

The European Health Insurance Card was approved by union ministers in Luxembourg to be in use by 2008, containing a range of data, including health files and records of treatment received. The original E111 form for the card was replaced in January 2006 with EHIC cards, and carried by 180 million Europeans by 2009.[17]

The head of State-watch, Tony Bunyan, said of the new ID cards, "We all know where they're heading with this. They want a single card with all our data on one chip. It'll be a passport and driver's license rolled into one with everything from our national insurance numbers, bank accounts, to health records."[18]

There has also been a "One Card" program proposed for North America. Documents from the SPP mention the creation of a North American ID card to facilitate cross border movement between the three countries. The One Card program would resemble a type of passport system, tracking the movement of citizens from all three countries.

The first step toward a North American ID card will likely be a U.S. national ID card. The Real ID Act of 2005, which would

---

16. "Blair Pleads Case for Biometric ID Cards," 2/20/2007, http://breitbart.com.
17. http://europa.eu/rapid/pressReleasesAction.do?reference=IP/09/1108&format=HTML&aged=0&language=EN&guiLanguage=en
18. Ambrose EvansPritchard, "Liberty Groups Attack Plan for EU Health ID Card," *London Telegraph*, http://telegraph.co.uk.

make mandatory a national ID card for every U.S. citizen, was easily passed by the U.S. House of Representatives, and in 2007 it was finally passed by the Senate when it was attached to a defense spending bill later signed into law by President Bush. The language of the act is vague and gives the Secretary of Homeland Security great leeway in regulating the new ID card, and determining what states will need to do to be in compliance with the law. Subsection 2 of the Act says, "The secretary shall determine whether a state is meeting the requirements of this section based on certifications made by the state to the Secretary."[19] The required certifications will be made in a manner determined solely by the Secretary of Homeland Security.

There is no specific requirement for a person's ethnicity, religion, or political affiliation to be placed on the card; however, many people are concerned with a requirement found in Title 11, Section 201, Subsection 9, which suggests the use of "a common machine-readable technology, with defined minimum data elements." Once again, the Secretary of Homeland Security will have full control over what that technology might be. Considering current international agreements to work together on RFID technology, RFID is the most likely choice. Already found in our passports, embedded RFID chips in a national ID card could contain any information the Secretary of Homeland Security deems relevant to fighting the war on terror, protecting the homeland, streamlining nationalized healthcare, or fighting illegal immigration. It's also worth thinking about that religion happens to be an important part of fighting the global war on terror. While it may not be politically correct to speak publicly about our intelligence service's monitoring of Muslim communities, mosques, and Muslim immigrants, the number of foiled terror plots across the United States since 9/11 indicates they are doing just that, and doing it successfully. A national ID card, identifying the religious preference of every citizen in the United

19. Brian McLain, "Fast Track to Tyranny: The REAL ID Act of 2005," 10/04/2007, http://www.411mania.com.

States, would be a much more effective way to monitor possible terrorist cells. A person's religious preference is already a part of their medical records, as anyone who's gone through the admitting process while checking into a hospital knows. It makes sense then that a national ID card, used for a future national healthcare system, will likely contain such information as well. One more piece of the puzzle fits neatly into place.

RFID technology would be a powerful tool in the hands of the Antichrist, but RFID alone will not allow the False Prophet to control and monitor commerce on a global scale. Another technological advance introduced in the 70s, called smart card technology, will not only complete the necessary components of the mark, but it has been slowly conditioning consumers around the world to accept a system of payment that can be easily monitored and controlled by a national, regional, and then a global government. The first use of "smart cards" by a large population of people was in France, where the Telecarte was used in French pay phones, starting in 1983. It was later used in French debit cards (Carte Bleue) in 1992.[20]

Smart cards look like any ordinary credit card, but they also contain an embedded RFID microchip that holds the consumer's personal and account information. When paying with a smart card, one inserts the card into the merchant's terminal and enters a security PIN (personal identification number) known only to the consumer and the bank that issued the card. Since the introduction of Carte Bleue, smart card use has exploded around the globe in the form of debit cards, electronic purses, and other forms of automatic payment systems.

Electronic purse systems eliminate the need for a bank account by storing the prepaid value of the card on the microchip. This also eliminates the need for a network that can connect to a bank or credit card company's system. This form of smart card has been used in numerous countries across Europe.[21]

---

20. Smart Card, Wikipedia, 3/13/07, http://en.wikipedia.org /wiki/Smart_card.
21. Ibid.

Technology progressed further still in the 90s, and smart card technology was applied to cell phones with the creation of the subscriber identity module, or SIM, allowing consumers to make purchases from their phones. With the pervasive use of cell phones across Europe, this put smart card and RFID technology in the hands of a vast percentage of the population.

In 1993, MasterCard, Visa, and Europay joined forces to develop smart cards that could be used as either debit or credit cards. The issuance of debit cards, and use of point-of-sale equipment exploded across Europe, and is now growing in popularity and use in the United States, albeit at a slower pace. The benefit to merchants, international payment brands, and banks is minimal, mostly reducing fraud and counterfeiting, rather than saving a great deal of money. It can, however, be argued that greater convenience leads to more impulse buying. Many in the payment industry believe the United States is waiting out the debit card phase in favor of a future contactless system of RFID payment, much like the contactless payment systems being used in mass transit. Mass transit systems in some larger cities allow smart cards to be used without removing them from your wallet or purse. This contactless technology is already being introduced into passports, patient card schemes, and identification cards as well.[22]

Some states in the U.S., like Vermont and Washington State, have even agreed to work with Homeland Security to test RFID driver's licenses. This is further evidence that the Department of Homeland Security will look to RFID technology when establishing guidelines for implementation of the Real ID Act.[23]

Smart cards are also becoming commonplace in healthcare systems, especially in Mexico and countries in South America. In the United States the Health Insurance Portability and Accountability Act (HIPPA), which placed greater responsibility

---

22. Ibid.
23. Orr Shtuh, "California May Ban Forced RFID Implants," *Central Valley Business Times*, September 20, 2007, http://www.centralvalleybusinesstimes.com.

on healthcare providers to keep patient information confidential and private, has fueled the use of smart cards for patient records in doctors offices and hospitals. The use of smart cards is saving the healthcare industry a great deal of money that, in the past, was spent on paper, ink, and the administrative cost of processing and archiving an enormous number of forms and patient records. Smart card technology will also help eliminate fraud in insurance claims and billing, a serious problem for most of the health care industry and the government.[24]

There are many reasons to link a national ID smart card system with nationalized health care. Nationalized healthcare will create a behemoth government bureaucracy charged with keeping patient records for millions of people. The current system of recording and archiving patient records would never support the massive data generated by hospitals, HMOs, doctors' offices, insurance companies, and government offices that would need to be integrated into one system. A smart card holding each patient's records and personal information on one microchip is the best, and perhaps the only, answer to such a huge undertaking. It is also an ideal selling point for a national ID card that has thus far been opposed unanimously by civil liberties groups around the world.

The ability to manage large amounts of data efficiently isn't the only justification for using smart cards in health care, however. Storing a patient's records on a microchip that can be read by any doctor and in any hospital in the country would eliminate the problem of "doctor shopping," a tactic used by drug abusers and addicts to get prescriptions for controlled substances from multiple different doctors without being detected. It would also reduce errors in prescribing by allowing physicians to access a patient's record of allergies and drug interactions in situations where communication with the patient isn't possible.

---

24. "Smart Cards in U.S. Healthcare: Benefits for Patients, Providers and Payers," Smart Card Alliance, 2/2007, http://www. Smartcardalliance.org.

Smart card technology is being used extensively in Mexico and South America, with over 30 percent of all bank cards in Mexico already using smart card technology. Mexico expects all bank cards to be replaced with smart cards by 2008. Brazil has already made 98 percent of all payment terminals in the country smart card ready, and experts estimate that Latin American countries have increased spending on this technology by 70 percent over the last year. There have also been new advances in contactless and mobile payments, making payment technologies a hot business in that region.[25]

This rapid spread of RFID and card technologies in Mexico and South America prompted the "Smart Card Alliance" to host a "Smart Cards for Government and Payment" conference in Mexico City in 2007. Government leaders met to discuss new ways to secure identification credentials, and learn about the latest developments in smart card technology. Also discussed were future technologies that will be far more advanced and capable of storing and managing data, and tracking and identifying the movement of assets, and even people. Attendees came away from the conference with many examples of uses for smart cards in their own country, including the Mexico Health Card, and the U.S. Department of Defense Common Access Card.[26]

Day two of the conference focused on contactless payment systems that are capable of debiting a person's account without any interaction with the buyer, requiring only that they pass within a certain range of an antenna. This technology, and even more advanced technology that we will explore shortly, represents the groundwork for the Mark of the Beast. As we're beginning to see, many current technologies already make controlling commerce on a global scale completely possible, feasible, and even necessary in an increasingly linked global economy. .

---

25. "Global Platform and Smart Card Alliance to Cohost 'Smart Cards for Government and Payment' Conference in Mexico City," Smart Card Alliance, 3/13/2007, http://www.smartcardalliance.org.
26. Ibid.

The Implantable Chip

The final technological advance that will take RFID and smart card technology to the next level is the implantable chip. Microchips made to be implanted in live human beings will be the inevitable next step in the creation of a stable cashless system of payment. The amazing thing is that this technology not only already exists, but chips are already being used to track our pets, monitor Alzheimer patients in assisted living facilities, and even in employees who work for large corporations as a means for controlling access to secure buildings.

Implantable RFID tags are tiny, data-storing microchips about the size of a grain of rice. Unlike the GPS technology we will look at next, RFID chips are scanned at close range as the "micro-chipped" person passes through a transponder unit at a checkpoint, or as they are scanned with a wand containing an antenna. There are currently 2,000 such chips implanted in humans according to Verichip Corp. of Delray Beach, Florida, the only implantable chip manufacturer with FDA approval. They are being used to store medical information, track the movement of patients with mental health or memory problems, and for gaining access to locked rooms or buildings. Verichip is focusing most heavily, however, on medical patient identification.[27]

Mandatory chipping of humans, such as personnel and patients, has been rare due to protests from civil liberty groups, but, like any new technology, chip makers are marketing their product with this in mind. As chips are accepted in smart cards, toll systems, and eventually in grocery stores, people will become used to the convenience and it will no longer be seen as an intrusion into their lives. Concerns about privacy will dwindle, just as the public backlash died down when consumers became used to the idea of RFID tags in their merchandise. By the time America catches up with Mexico

---

27. "Smart Card Alliance : News, Global Platform and Smart Card Alliance to Co-host 'Smart Cards for Government and Payment' Conference in Mexico City, Princeton Junction, NJ, and Foster City, CA," 3/13/07, http://www. smartcardalliance.org.

and South America in smart card technology and national biometric identification cards, RFID will be as widely accepted as cell phones, blackberries, and global positioning systems in cars.

Applied Digital Solutions, the parent company of Verichip, Corp., has suggested that the implantable chip could also be injected through a syringe and used as a sort of "human bar code" in security applications. Applied Digital has estimated that the market for implantable chips could reach as much as $70 billion a year. Paul Saffo, a director of the Institute for the Future was quoted in 2002 as saying, "Are we going to see chips embedded in the human body? You bet we are, but it isn't going to happen overnight." That year they sold millions of dollars worth of Verichips, with the largest market being in South America and Europe where they are leaps and bounds ahead of the United States in chip technology and RFID systems. Implantable chips are big business, and they are increasingly being accepted by the general population.[28]

Interestingly, the first human chip was implanted in a New Jersey surgeon, Richard Seeling. Dr. Seeling was motivated to try it after seeing the images of New York firefighters at the World Trade Center on 9/11 writing their social security numbers on their forearms with magic markers, so they could be identified if they were killed during the rescue effort. Implanting chips in humans would be a huge benefit to rescue and recovery workers, firefighters, police, and medical examiners during rescue operations, especially following a natural disaster. Families would no longer have to wait weeks for medical examiners to compare dental records in order to identify their loved ones, as we saw happen following 9/11 and Hurricane Katrina. Similarly, the military could benefit from replacing "dog tags" with implantable chips, making the identification of casualties during war instant, and with far less risk of errors.

The failed recovery mission following Hurricane Katrina made an excellent case for better forms of identification. A national ID

---

28. Orr Shtuh, "California May Ban Forced RFID Implants," *Central Valley Business Times*, 9/20/07, http://www.centralvalleybusinesstimes.com.

system would have made FEMA's job of distributing funds and determining where resources were needed far easier. It would also greatly reduce the number of fraudulent payments, scams, and people who always fall through the cracks during a natural disaster response.

Applied Digital expects the chips to be used in a variety of RFID applications, including security, and in fighting the war on terror. When you consider the integration of global positioning systems (GPS) with the chips, the possibilities become endless, and the mark of the beast becomes a real possibility for our future.

RFID chips with GPS technology manufactured by Digital Angel Corporation are already being used in high value assets, military and civilian aircraft, and in millions of pets in the United States and Europe. Livestock are being physically tracked with these systems throughout their life cycle. Outer Link's Comm Track™ communication center software allows commercial fleets to be monitored and tracked in graphical formats over the Internet. If assets and pets can be tracked anywhere in the world, humans can also be tracked. In fact, they already are.

We've all seen the reports on national news broadcasts of missing children, spouses, and friends, and heard the family members plead with whoever abducted their loved one to return them safely. In response to this national tragedy, Congress passed "Amber's Law" creating Amber Alerts, which now go out over the airwaves, on electronic billboards, and national and local network newscasts within hours of a child abduction. Amber Alerts have saved lives, and brought numerous children home safely who might otherwise have been lost forever, but there are still far too many who are never found. Parents are responding to this rise in crime against children by buying book bags and other retail items that are equipped with GPS technology capable of locating their children anywhere in the world, and at any time.

A system operated by the security firm Secom Co., has created a backpack with satellite tracking technology that allows parents to view the location of their children from a website, which uses satellite technology to track the GPS system integrated into the bag.

In 2003, GPS technology was also tested for use in human implants. Applied Digital Solutions took RFID chip technology to the next level by successfully field-testing a prototype of a GPS implant for humans. The implanted chip allows a person to be tracked by GPS, and the information relayed wirelessly to the Internet where the individual's location, movements, and vital signs can be accessed or stored in a database for later use. The biggest obstacle thus far, aside from the outcry coming from privacy rights groups, is the size of the unit, which is about the size of a pacemaker. However, Applied Digital believes it will be able to perfect the technology to a point where the chip will be easily implanted in any human being.

Applied Digital has suggested that the market for GPS chips would be potential hostage targets and outdoorsmen who want to be found. However, any RFID system could easily be migrated to a GPS-enabled system as consumers and the public become more accepting of the technology and events like terrorist attacks make people more willing to give up their privacy and freedoms in the name of security. In fact, the U.S. government has already expressed an interest in utilizing the technology in high-risk parolees who are released from prison.

All of these areas of technological advance in conjunction with global agreements are coming together to fulfill what the Bible prophesies will happen in the end times. Nations are giving up their national sovereignty in favor of regional governments, and the European Union is leading the way, just as the Bible said it would.

RFID technology is being integrated into global commerce by world leaders who know that a cashless society is the only way government can have full control. It's not just a coincidence that, at the same time, global positioning technology, national biometric identification cards, and government-controlled healthcare are all being legislated and accepted by populations that would have balked at this invasion into their privacy just a decade ago.

With natural disasters increasing every year, terrorist attacks threatening peace around the globe, and the European Union gaining power globally through regional integration, it's only a matter of time before the rest of the world throws caution to the wind in order to keep up. The United States will have to regionalize to compete, and our system of commerce will have to follow the example of the revived Roman Empire of end-times Scripture, if we are to survive as a country. With each region following the E.U.'s lead, the Antichrist will have but to globalize what has already been done on a regional basis. The False Prophet will indeed be able to use existing and future technology to monitor every transaction and every person on the planet, and forbid any person who refuses to take the mark from buying or selling.

Chapter 9

THE GLORIOUS APPEARING

There has been no shortage of movies coming out of Hollywood that bring the utter annihilation of the planet to the big screen. In fact, many people today believe that our world is on a collision course with destruction. Whether it is global warming, irresponsible stewardship of our natural resources, or nuclear war, they see an end to our existence and the death of the planet as a certainty. Sadly, a large majority of people won't recognize that end until it's too late. Those who choose to follow the Antichrist and believe his lies during the Tribulation won't see the peril that lies before them, and will stand with him in the Valley of Megiddo for a final battle between good and evil. As we'll see in this chapter, the victory belonged to Jesus long before we were even spoken into existence.

The Antichrist's reign over the earth will last exactly seven years, and his evil plan will culminate in a final battle between good and evil. At that time the Lord will return in the air with the saints to do battle with the Antichrist and all those who chose to follow the Beast and take his mark. Revelation 19 describes this final battle, as the Tribulation period comes to a close. The chapter begins with the roaring sound of the multitudes in heaven shouting "Hallelujah," and praising God. It's a joyous and celebratory time in heaven because the curtain is about to open to God's final judgment on earth, and the long awaited glorious appearing of Christ. God will finally avenge the blood of the martyred saints, and condemn the great prostitute for her sins against God. Standing together in heaven, the Old Testament saints and all those who accepted Christ during the Church Age will gather around their Savior, who sits on His throne in heaven, preparing to reign over His Kingdom on earth.

The Joyous Judgment of the Saints

While there is some debate about the timing of Christ's judgment for the saints of all ages, Scripture seems to indicate that we will stand before Christ to be judged at some point during this celebration in heaven, just prior to the marriage supper of the Lamb. Revelation 19 says that the Bride of Christ (the Church) will be made ready through her righteous acts, and Ephesians 5:27 also indicates that the bride will be presented to the Bridegroom (Jesus) "without stain or wrinkle, or any other blemish, but holy and blameless." We must conclude, then, that this state of perfection is achieved by the judgment of each person's works at the judgment seat of Christ, before the Bride is presented to Jesus during the marriage supper of the Lamb.

Second Corinthians 5:9–10 says, "So we make it our goal to please him, whether we are at home in the body or away from it. For we must all appear before the judgment seat of Christ, that each may receive what is due him for the things done while in the body, whether good or bad."

Many Christians aren't aware that we will all face a time of judgment before our Savior. Churches and pastors spend a great deal of time reassuring believers that their sins have been forgiven and salvation is a free gift. Indeed, it is. However, the Bible also says that faith without works is dead. Our works and the way we live our lives matters a great deal, and our reward in heaven depends on how Christ-like we are while in the body. This isn't a comfortable topic for some in the Church, and they often don't want to hear about consequences, or the expectations God has for us. They prefer, instead, to hear a sermon that gives them the warm fuzzies and makes them feel secure in their salvation no matter how they might be living their lives. Sadly, many leaders in the Church neglect their duty to their congregations to make them aware of the judgment they will one day face. It's easier to focus on God's judgment of all unbelievers, which will take place at the end of the Millennial Kingdom. Perhaps if the importance of our works were given greater emphasis along with the reward that awaits us in heaven, there would be far less hypocrisy found in the Body of Christ today.

Ecclesiastes 12:14 says that God will judge us for everything we do, including every secret thing, whether good or bad. While every single person who ever lives will be judged at some point after they die, the judgment for believers is different, and has a far more desirable outcome than that of unbelievers. For those who aren't saved, the final judgment is a time of great sorrow, where the death penalty is meted out to pay for the sins of those who didn't accept Christ's sacrifice (Romans 6:23). But, for believers it *should* be a time of reward for their service to God (Matthew 25:14-30). However, there will be those who will have to face the realities of a life that should have been lived more in keeping with God's Word. For them, there may not be much of a reward. It's important to point out, however, that while some people will receive no reward for a selfish life devoid of any evidence of their salvation, the judgment seat will not be a time of condemnation. Romans 8:1, tells us that "there is no condemnation for those who belong to Christ Jesus." Our judgment is for the purposes of receiving commendation rather than condemnation.

First Corinthians 4:4–5 says, "It is the Lord who judges me. Therefore judge nothing before the appointed time; wait till the Lord comes. He will bring to light what is hidden in darkness and will expose the motives of men's hearts. At that time *each will receive his praise from God*" (emphasis added).

Our sins have been forgiven once and for all by the sacrifice Christ made on the Cross. Those sins need not be paid for again at the judgment seat. However, our actions, thoughts, and the way we lived our lives will be brought out into the light and judged by Christ Himself. This should make all of us want to live a life we can be proud of, rather than ashamed of. How many things in our lives would we do differently, if we lived as if our decisions and actions were being recorded in a book that would be read back to us when our lives are finished? That's exactly what is going to happen.

Jesus had this time of judgment in mind when He instructed us in Matthew 6:20 to store up for ourselves treasures in heaven. There is no reward for how rich we become in our lives on earth, or how many possessions we acquire. Instead, we are to be rewarded for what we did for Jesus and the furtherance of the gospel in the short time we have here on earth. Second Timothy 2:12 says that, if we endure trials and struggles on earth the way Jesus told us to, we will reign with Him when He returns at the end of the Tribulation. How we reign, and in what position of authority is dependent upon how well we endure now.

The parable of the ten minas in Luke 19:11–26 explains God's purpose for this system of rewarding our righteous acts. Luke writes in these verses that ten servants were given one mina each before their master embarked on a journey to become king over a distant land. When the master returned, he called his servants together and asked them to make an accounting of what they'd done with the mina they were given. The first servant reported that he had invested his mina, and multiplied it by ten. Each successive servant had done less than the one before, until the final servant presented only one mina — the same mina he had been given before his master left. He stood before his master and confessed that he had done nothing with what he had been given. When the king judged the servants and handed down their reward for their efforts while he was away, the servant who had ten minas was given charge of ten cities in the king's kingdom. Each servant was given charge of a number of cities according to the number of minas they had presented to the king upon his return. All but the last servant, that is, who was given nothing. Because he had done nothing with what he was given, he was given no authority in the king's kingdom, and his mina was taken away and given to the servant who had done the most.

Matthew 13:12 says, "Whoever has, will be given more, and he will have an abundance. Whoever does not have, even what he has will be taken from him." So it will be when Christ judges the saints before He returns with them to reign over His Millennial Kingdom. How we reign and what authority and privilege we're given in the Kingdom will depend on what we do now. What will you receive from your Lord on the Day of Judgment? I hope it will be a great reward for work well done, but the reality is, there will be many of us who are left disappointed and ashamed.

The Marriage Supper of the Lamb

Following Christ's purification of His Bride through the judgment of the saints, we will all be invited to the marriage supper of the Lamb. Revelation 19:7–9 explains the marriage supper this way:

> Let us rejoice and be glad and give him glory! For the wedding of the Lamb has come, and his bride has made herself ready. Fine linen, bright and clean, was given her to wear. (Fine linen stands for the righteous acts of the saints.) Then the angel said to me, "Write: 'Blessed are those who are invited to the wedding supper of the Lamb!' " And he added, "These are the true words of God."

Jesus used marriage suppers more than once in his parables. In the case of the marriage supper of the Lamb, Jesus is of course the Lamb of God, and He is also the Bridegroom at this wedding celebration in heaven. John 3:29 refers to Jesus as the Bridegroom, and the identity of the Bride is given to us in Ephesians 5:32 when Paul refers to the Church as the Bride of Christ. God also says in

2 Corinthians 11:2, "I am jealous for you with a godly jealousy. I promised you to one husband, to Christ, so that I might present you as a pure virgin to him."

In addition to a Bride and Bridegroom, there will also be guests attending the wedding. Revelation 19:9 refers to those who will be invited to the wedding supper. We know these guests can't be the Church, because the bride is never a guest at her own wedding. In John 3:29 John the Baptist is named as one of these friends of the Bridegroom, which tells us that the Bride's guests at the wedding are the Old Testament saints who lived and died before Christ's sacrifice on the Cross. Those who put their faith in the God of the Bible in the Old Testament will be honored and blessed to be invited to the wedding. This doesn't mean, however, that the Old Testament saints are in any way inferior or less important to God than those who accepted Christ after His sacrifice on the Cross. All believers will receive their reward at the appointed time, and they will have their own special relationship with the Lamb. The Jewish believers of the Old Testament were, after all, God's chosen people, and they will surely have a special place in the hierarchy of believers in heaven.

It was customary in biblical times to have a reception following a wedding, much like we do today. The reception following the marriage supper of the Lamb will be a glorious time when all of heaven will celebrate the long-awaited return of Christ. On earth, the seven-year Tribulation will be coming to a close. After three and a half years of judgments on the wicked who chose to follow the Antichrist, the Tribulation will culminate in a final battle between those left on earth and all those in attendance at the celebration in heaven, who will be joined by the Tribulation saints. Jesus will return to earth the same way He came, but with the saints of all ages accompanying him. Matthew 24:29–31 describes the return of Christ this way: "Immediately after the distress of those days, the sun will be darkened, and the moon will not give its light; the stars will fall from the sky, and the heavenly bodies will be shaken. At that time the sign of the Son of Man will appear in the sky, and all the nations of the earth will mourn. They will see the Son of Man coming on the clouds of the sky, with power and great glory. And he will send his angels with a loud trumpet call, and they will gather his elect from the four winds, from one end of the heavens to the other."

The Rapture, Part Two

This event is a kind of second installment of the Rapture. When the Lord returns in the air, everyone on the planet will see him. Believers will rejoice, because they will know their time of waiting is over, and their Lord is coming to destroy the Antichrist and his armies, and reign over the earth. Those believers who accepted Christ at some point after the Rapture, and during the Tribulation period, will be gathered together and raptured in much the same way that the Church was raptured seven years prior. Some people have mistakenly interpreted these verses as evidence that the Rapture doesn't happen until the very end of the Tribulation, meaning believers will not be spared the judgments and wrath of God on earth that will mark the last half of the Tribulation. However, we know this can't be a description of the Rapture of the Church, because the return of Christ is not described in this way when the Church is raptured. During the Rapture of the Church, believers are snatched away into heaven to be with the Lord. The Tribulation saints will meet the Lord in the air as He's returning. Furthermore, as we just learned, the marriage supper of the Lamb has just taken place in heaven. So the Church must have been raptured already, making it possible for them to return with Christ during the glorious appearing. In other words, the Church has obviously already been raptured and has taken part in the festivities in heaven when this second installment of the Rapture takes place.

With all of the believers from all ages, as well as those saved during the Tribulation gathered around Him, Christ will return to an earth that is peopled totally with the unsaved. Those who rejected Christ's offer of salvation will stand with the Antichrist as Jesus returns with the saints to execute a final judgment on the wicked. Enoch prophesied about the returning saints in Jude 1:14–15 when he said, "See, the Lord is coming with thousands upon thousands of his holy ones to judge everyone, and to convict all the ungodly of all the ungodly acts they have done in the ungodly way, and of all the harsh words ungodly sinners have spoken against him."

The Battle of Armageddon

We've all probably heard of the battle of Armageddon. There have been movies made about it, and previous wars have been compared to this future battle throughout history. However, there has never truly been a war like the one that will end the Antichrist's authority on earth. The final battle when Christ returns really will be the war to end all wars.

It's a common misperception that the battle of Armageddon is executed as one large battle between good and evil. However, it is actually a label for the sum total of several battles that will take place in a single day when Christ returns. The following chart describes the battles that will make up the battle of Armageddon.

The final battle on the great day of the Lord will be waged in Jerusalem. The Antichrist, indwelt by Satan, will rally his forces to make one last attempt to destroy God's city. Satan will be defeated a final time, and his armies destroyed.

Following these battles, the only evil left to be conquered by Christ will be the False Prophet, Satan, and his host, the Antichrist. Revelation 20 describes the end of the Beast and his co-deceiver first.

> But the beast was captured, and with him the false prophet who had performed the miraculous signs on his behalf. With these signs he had deluded those who had received the mark of the beast and worshiped his image. The two of them were thrown alive into the fiery lake of burning sulfur (Revelation 19:20).

BATTLE	SCRIPTURE	DESCRIPTION
The Battle of Armageddon	Revelation 16:12–16; Ezekiel 39:17–22; Revelation 19:15	Jesus will be victorious in a battle against the Antichrist's armies in the Valley of Megiddo.
The Battle of the Valley of Jehoshaphat	Joel 3:1–2, 9–17; Revelation 14:14–20	Armies from other nations will battle Christ in the Valley of Jehoshaphat. Jesus will reap a judgment harvest on the nations of the earth for their persecution of the nation of Israel.
The Battle of Jerusalem	Zechariah 12:1–9; Revelation 16:17–21	The final battle on the Great Day of the Lord will be waged in Jerusalem. The Antichrist, indwelt by Satan, will rally his forces to make one last attempt to destroy God's city. Satan will be defeated a final time, and his armies destroyed.

The Judgment of the Antichrist and False Prophet

So the Antichrist and False Prophet will finally meet their demise in a fiery lake of burning sulfur. Satan, however, won't be thrown into the lake of fire with the Antichrist and False Prophet, but will be bound and put out of commission for 1,000 years, during which time Jesus will reign over the Millennial Kingdom on earth. This new kingdom that will be established after Christ returns to defeat

Satan, will be the utopia so many generations tried and failed to create. What politicians, governments, and nations couldn't build will be established over a period of days by our Savior and King.

When Jesus has judged the Antichrist, the False Prophet, and Satan, and his armies have been defeated, Jesus will judge everyone on earth. The Tribulation saints, who are the believers martyred for their faith by the Antichrist, will be raised to life and will stand below the altar at Jesus' feet. The rest of the believers from throughout time will stand at the right hand of Christ, while the goats, or those who rejected Christ and either died or lived through the Tribulation without being saved, will stand on the left side of Christ. Jesus will be surrounded by billions of people who had a choice to make during their lives, and they will now either go on to rule with Christ in the Millennial Kingdom, or suffer eternal damnation. It is at this time that the unbelievers will receive their punishment for their wickedness and for rejecting Christ. The actual judgment of the goats will take place at the end of the Millennium, as we will discuss later.

> When the Son of Man comes in his glory, and all the angels with him, he will sit on his throne in heavenly glory. All the nations will be gathered before him, and he will separate the people one from another as a shepherd separates the sheep from the goats. He will put the sheep on his right and the goats on his left. Then the King will say to those on his right, "Come, you who are blessed by my Father; take your inheritance, the kingdom prepared for you since the creation of the world. . . ." Then he will say to those on his left, "Depart from me, you who are cursed, into the eternal fire prepared for the devil and his angels" (Matthew 25:31–41).

Those who chose to reject Christ and persecute the saints will be cast into hell for eternity, leaving only those who followed Christ to join Him as He reigns with His Church in the Millennial Kingdom.

The Triple Destruction of the Earth

The Bible tells us that the earth will be destroyed a total of three times. Our planet was first destroyed during Noah's time with a great Flood that wiped out all but Noah, his family, and the animals preserved on the ark. The second renovation of our planet will take place just prior to the start of Christ's millennial reign. Isaiah 65:17 says, "Behold, I will create new heavens and a new earth. The former things will not be remembered, nor will they come to mind." This verse comes right before a description of the Millennial Kingdom, and describes a time when Jesus will remake the earth into a paradise, much like the Garden of Eden before the Fall of man. The Apostle Peter predicted this time of great change on earth that will immediately follow the day of the Lord in 2 Peter 3:1–16. During this renovation, the earth's surface will be completely destroyed, leaving Jesus with a fresh canvas to create a beautiful new earth for His Church. Peter says in verse 11, "Since everything will be destroyed in this way, what kind of people ought you to be? You ought to live holy and godly lives as you look forward to the day of God."

The third such destruction of the planet and the heavens will take place after the thousand year reign of Christ, when God will create an entirely new earth in preparation for the New Jerusalem, where believers will dwell for eternity. We'll discuss this new earth in greater detail later in the chapter. We know that the renovation of the earth described in Isaiah and 2 Peter is not a reference to the new earth that is described in Revelation 21:1, because the verses in Isaiah speak of death and the judgment of the nations, and 2 Peter refers to the timing as being during the "day of the Lord." The day of the Lord and Christ's judgment of the nations happen before the Millennial Kingdom, therefore there must be two separate events that take place, before and then after the Millennium.

During the Millennial Kingdom

The Millennial Kingdom will be populated by the believers from throughout the ages, as well as those who were raptured in their earthly bodies and have not yet died. Isaiah 65:20 says of the Millennial Kingdom, "Never again will there be in it an infant who lives but a few days, or an old man who does not live out his years; he who dies at a hundred will be thought a mere youth; he who fails to reach one hundred will be considered accursed." With Satan bound in the great abyss for the Millennium, the only temptation people will face during this time is the temptation of the flesh, and that only applies to those who came into the Millennium in the flesh, because they did not die an earthly death before or during the great day of the Lord. These people will live out their lives during the Millennium, have children, and populate the Millennial Kingdom with new generations of people. Those who had already died and were given their glorified bodies will reign with Christ over this new earth for one thousand years. Verse 20 seems to indicate that there will be no death from sickness or the other tragedies that often take our loved ones from us in this imperfect, sinful world we now live in. People will live long lives, much like people did during the period of time from Adam and Eve through the Great Flood. In fact, those alive in the flesh when the Millennium begins, as well as those who are born and accept Christ during the Millennium will live the entire 1,000 years before receiving their glorified bodies. Because of the expanded life spans of those still in the flesh, there will be a huge population explosion on the planet. Women will have children into their hundreds, and a person who reaches one hundred years old will be considered young! Couples will also be able to have as many children as they want, because they will no longer need to worry about how they will feed and care for such a large family. There will be an abundance of food, and Jesus will provide for our every need. In addition to unprecedented blessings on earth, billions of other believers will be willing to help care for the youngest among them. However, this verse also indicates that even under the best circumstances imaginable, not everyone will accept the free gift of salvation through belief in Christ.

Those born during the Millennium will have to use their free will to make a choice for Christ, just as all believers have had to do since Christ's death on the Cross. In a peaceful world without Satan's influence on people's lives, most people will indeed choose to follow Christ early in life. However, even in the Millennial Kingdom, there will be those who choose to arrogantly reject Christ and follow their own desires. During the life of each of these unbelievers they will, no doubt, propagate a generation of unbelievers who will willingly follow Satan when he is released from the Abyss where he remains chained until the end of the Millennium (Revelation 20:7). You might have been wondering why Satan was only bound in chains, while the Antichrist and False Prophet were thrown into the lake of fire. This is because Satan will be loosed one final time at the end of the Millennium to rebel against the Lord and those who have rejected Christ will stand with Satan in a final battle. They will be defeated, of course, along with Satan himself.

After the Millennial Kingdom

At the end of the Millennial Kingdom, those who died without accepting Christ will finally receive their own judgment and punishment for the life they chose apart from God. Revelation 20:5 says, "The rest of the dead did not come to life until the thousand years were ended." The rest of the dead are those who died without accepting Christ, or in the case of those who lived before Christ's sacrifice, died without faith in the God of Abraham, Isaac, and Jacob. This will also include those who were cast into the lake of fire at the end of the Tribulation. The Great White Throne judgment is reserved for these unbelievers, and is described in Revelation 20:11–12.

> Then I saw a great white throne and him who was seated on it. Earth and sky fled from his presence, and there was no place for them. And I saw the dead, great and small, standing before the throne, and books were opened. Another book

was opened, which is the book of life. The dead were judged according to what they had done as recorded in the books.

The White Throne Judgment is for those who never accepted Christ and died in their sin, or had not accepted Christ when He returned with the Church. Verses 13 and 14 say, "The Sea gave up the dead that were in it, and death and Hades gave up the dead that were in them, and each person was judged according to what he had done. Then death and Hades were thrown into the lake of fire." Just as believers were judged for their works and service to Christ, the dead will be resurrected, united with their soul, which has been waiting in eternal torment, and stand before Christ to be judged.

Judgment of the condemned's works is followed by judgment from the book of life (Revelation 20:15). This is referring to the Lamb's book of life, not the book of life that all names are written in. If a person's name isn't found in the book of life, and of course it won't be in the case of these unbelievers, they are cast into the lake of fire for eternity. You might be wondering why unbelievers would have their works judged, if they are already condemned. Remember, the Bible tells us that we will ALL have to make an accounting for what we do with our lives on earth. This includes those who didn't accept Christ, as well.

At this point God's righteous judgment will have been worked out with every single person who ever lived. All that is left is for all of the believers from before the glorious appearing, and throughout the Millennial Kingdom to begin what will be their eternity with God.

When you hear someone speak of going to heaven after they die, they are referring to their soul, which will leave the body and reside in heaven until Christ's return. At the glorious appearing, Christians are returned to their new glorified bodies. Our eternity will be spent in these glorified bodies on a new earth with God. Revelation 21 introduces us to the world that will be ours for eternity. This perfectly beautiful, new world is what God had in mind for us all along, and it is what Jesus was speaking of when He said, "In my Father's house are many rooms. . . . I am going there to prepare a place for you" (John 14:2). The old earth, which had been renovated twice already, will be completely destroyed this time, and a new heaven and earth will take its place. At this point, Jesus will turn the Kingdom over to God the Father.

> Then the end will come, when he hands over the kingdom to God the Father after he has destroyed all dominion, authority and power. For he must reign until he has put all his enemies under his feet. The last enemy to be destroyed is death. For he "has put everything under his feet." Now when it says that "everything" has been put under him, it is clear that this does not include God himself, who put everything under Christ. When he has done this, then the Son himself will be made subject to him who put everything under him, so that God may be all in all (1 Corinthians 15:24–28).

Once authority has been handed over to God the Father, God will bring down from heaven the New Jerusalem where we, His children, will dwell with God for eternity. Imagine that! We mere humans will live in the New Jerusalem with the God that created the universe! And what luxury and happiness we will experience in this New Jerusalem, prepared just for us.

Chapters 21 and 22 of Revelation list seven specific things that will make up our existence for eternity. There will be a new heaven (21:1), a new earth (21:1), a new Jerusalem (21:2), new things (21:5), a new place for God's throne (22:3), and a new source of light, which will be the Lord Himself (22:5). So bright will be the light provided by the presence of God, there will be no day and night, and no need for any other light source anywhere.

As I stated earlier, at the end of the one thousand year reign of Christ, the earth and heavens will be destroyed a third time and replaced with a new heaven and earth. Revelation 21:1 says, "Then

I saw a new heaven and a new earth, for the first heaven and the first earth had passed away, and there was no longer any sea." The earth was first destroyed by a flood and then by Jesus Himself as He restored it to its original glory, but the third time the earth is destroyed it won't consist of merely a resurfacing of the planet. It will be destroyed completely, along with the heavens, and an entirely new earth with no oceans will be created in its place. It will be better than anything we've ever known. It will be heaven on earth, in the same way that the Garden of Eden was prepared as a paradise for Adam and Eve. While none of the land masses will be wasted on oceans, probably to accommodate the billions of believers that will live there, it will have a river that will provide an abundance of water.

> I saw the Holy City, the new Jerusalem, coming down out of heaven from God, prepared as a bride beautifully dressed for her husband. And I heard a loud voice from the throne saying, "Now the dwelling of God is with men, and he will live with them. They will be his people, and God himself will be with them and be their God (Revelation 21:2–3).

How exciting to know that, as believers, we will spend eternity in paradise with God Himself! We will be living in the city that Jesus said He was going to prepare for us in John 14:1–3. What a loving God we have that He would prepare such an amazing city for us, and leave the third heaven to dwell on earth with His creation.

The Benefits of the New Jerusalem

Let's look a little closer at this New Jerusalem where we will be living with God for eternity.

> The angel who talked with me had a measuring rod of gold to measure the city, its gates and its walls. The city was laid out like a square, as long as it was wide. He measured

the city with the rod and found it to be 12,000 stadia in length, and as wide and high as it is long (Revelation 21:15–16).

To understand just how big this city will be, imagine a city that stretches from about the eastern seaboard of the United States all the way to the Mississippi River on one side, and from the Canadian border to the Gulf of Mexico on the other. Scripture tells us it will also be this distance in height! Tim LaHaye explains the New Jerusalem this way in his book *Revelation Unveiled*:

> Dr. Henry M. Morris, an expert engineer and author, has done the math on this and concluded that given the estimated population of a possible twenty billion residents, each person would enjoy a block of space of approximately one cubic mile, or its length, breadth, and height would be a little over a third of a mile in each direction.[1]

Imagine a cubic mile of space all to yourself, to enjoy the fellowship of your loved ones, worship God, and live in perfect peace in the most beautiful city ever built.

Apparently there will still be nations in this new world, because Revelation 21:22–24 says that God will be the light for the city, and the city the light for the nations. Perhaps we will be able to travel and enjoy the splendor of a world that was made to be a perfect paradise for God's people.

Even more exciting, God will maintain a fellowship with us, much like he did with Adam and Eve in the Garden of Eden. All of the believers from the beginning of the first earth through the end of the Millennial Kingdom will be able to commune with God. Revelation 21:4 says that God "will wipe every tear from their eyes. There will be no more death or mourning or crying or pain, for the old order of things has passed away." Never again will we lose

---

1. Tim LaHaye, *Revelation Unveiled* (Colorado Springs, CO: Alive Communications, 1999), p. 361.

a loved one to death or illness, or suffer any of the painful diseases and disabilities so common in our world today. This verse should also comfort any of us who know the pain of having a loved one that hasn't accepted Christ, and may not make it to the Millennial Kingdom and an eternity with God in the New Jerusalem. Perhaps we won't feel pain because we won't remember those loved ones, having been spared the memory supernaturally by God, or perhaps God will simply take our pain and replace it with joy and happiness. We can't know for certain how God will spare us that sadness, but this verse tells us that he most assuredly will. There will be no despair, grief, sadness, pain, guilt, temptation, or any other feeling that we suffered through in a world where Satan had the power to affect man's free will.

This unimaginable peace, happiness, and prosperity stands in stark contrast to what those who did not accept Christ will have to endure for eternity.

> But the cowardly, the unbelieving, the vile, the murderers, the sexually immoral, those who practice magic arts, the idolaters and all liars — their place will be in the fiery lake of burning sulfur. This is the second death (Revelation 21:8).

There is no second chance for these unfortunate souls who rejected the free gift of salvation Jesus offered to every one of us. If you are a believer, draw on the tremendous hope we can take from the eternity that awaits us, and do everything possible to bring as many people with you as you can. Live your lives in such a way that those around you will want to know the reason for the hope that is in you, and search people out who may want to know your God.

If you are an unbeliever, and haven't accepted Christ as your Savior and Lord, now is the time. Revelation 21:6 tells us that if you call on the name of Christ He will "give to drink without cost from the spring of the water of life." If you have any doubt about where you will spend eternity, Jesus is waiting to give you that assurance that you will spend eternity with Him in paradise. You need only believe in Him and ask. But don't wait too long. As we've seen in this book, the time of Christ's return is very near. Maybe today!

The Spirit and the bride say, "Come!" And let him who hears say, "Come!" Whoever is thirsty, let him come; and whoever wishes, let him take the free gift of the water of life (Revelation 22:17).

More from Dr. Gary Frazier

As president of Discovery Missions , Gary Frazier, a respected speaker and writer on the subject of Bible prophecy and current events, has appeared on numerous documentaries, the History Channel, and national radio programs. Authoring numerous books, he is a contributor to the LaHaye *Prophecy Study Bible* and *The Popular Encyclopedia of Bible Prophecy*, and travels nationally, speaking in many of America's largest churches.

More books from Dr. Frazier:

America at the Tipping Point

Signs of the Coming Christ

What Really Happens When Jesus Returns

discoverymissions.org

facebook.com/**drgaryfrazier**

twitter.com/**gdfrazier7**

If *It Could Happen Tomorrow* challenged and inspired you, please consider writing and posting a review at any online retailer.

What's next?

What will you do with the Bible's promise of the impending Second Coming of Christ?

Share your thoughts with Dr. Frazier and New Leaf Publishing Group here:

 MasterBooks
drgaryfrazier

 MasterBooks4u
gdfrazier7

It Could Happen Tomorrow is also available in digital format.

iBooks

Kindle

Nook

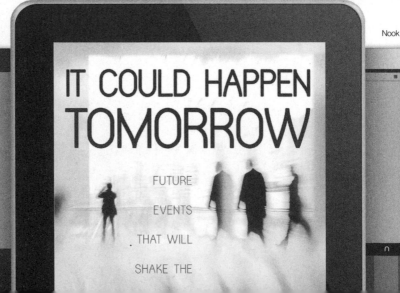

IT COULD HAPPEN TOMORROW

FUTURE

EVENTS

THAT WILL

SHAKE THE

Want to learn more about Biblical Prophecy?

Check out these titles:

nlpg.com

New Leaf Press
A Division of New Leaf Publishing Group